Elfrida

Swegn Forkbeard

The Redeless = Emma = CANUTE
1016 -1035

HARDICANUTE   HAROL...
1040 -1042   1035 -1040

EDWARD The Confessor   HAROLD
1042 -1066

e Conqueror

...eta = Stephen of Blois

...TEPHEN
1135 -1154

JOHN = Isabelle of Angouleme
1199 -1216

HENRY III = Eleanor of Provence
1216 -1272

PLANTAGENET

...lainault

Swynford   Edmund D. of York = Isabel of Castile

...orset = Margaret Holland   Richard E. of Cambridge = Anne Mortimer

...John Beaufort = Margaret Beauchamp   Richard D. of York = Cecily Neville

...t Beaufort

A THOUSAND YEARS OF
BRITISH MONARCHY

A Thousand Years of British Monarchy

SIR ARTHUR BRYANT

BOOK CLUB ASSOCIATES

This edition published by
Purnell Book Services Limited
by arrangement with William Collins

First published in a limited edition
by John Pinches Limited 1973
Published in this edition 1975

© John Pinches Limited, 1973

Set in Monotype Fontana
Made and printed in Great Britain by
William Collins Sons and Co. Ltd, Glasgow

FOREWORD

The credit for this study in miniature of our monarchy and its history belongs to John Pinches Limited, the distinguished medallists and the oldest private mint in the country. Three years ago, they invited me to direct the research for a special collection of sterling silver ingots to be issued to commemorate the thousandth anniversary of the coronation at Bath Abbey in AD 973 of the first acknowledged King of All England, Edgar I. I was also invited to write an explanatory volume to accompany the fifty ingot collection to be entitled *1000 Years of British Monarchy*.

The task set me was to describe in between 600 and 750 words – for a double page spread – the reign and the character of each of the fifty sovereigns who reigned over England – and since 1603 over Britain – between Edgar I and our present Queen. My first reaction was to regard the task as almost impossible in so small a compass. But having in my writings during the past forty years covered an unusually wide field of English history, I decided, with the help and encouragement of John Pinches Limited and their Managing Director, Mr Michael Golding, to treat their invitation as a challenge and, while trying to combine the requirements of historical balance and truth with those of popular interest and readability, to weave my brief accounts of each of the successive monarchs and reigns into what, in reality, they constitute a continuous history in miniature of the realm and of our country.

I should like, therefore, to express my gratitude to John Pinches Limited, their Chairman, Mr Brian Harrison, and my friend, Mike Golding, both for having commissioned, and so created, a book originally intended solely for collectors of their commemorative series, and for their generosity in allowing it now to be offered to a wider public. I am also much indebted to Miss Julia Halle for having helped me in the preparation of the biographies.

The Close, Salisbury
May 1975

ARTHUR BRYANT

INTRODUCTION

May 11th 1973 marked the thousandth anniversary of the coronation of King Edgar in Bath Abbey as the first King of all England. Since then, except during the eleven years of the Cromwellian interregnum, England has never been without a Sovereign, even though at times the Crown was contended for by rival claimants. It has descended, down to our own time, through those who have traced their descent from King Edgar and from his more famous great-grandfather, Alfred of Wessex. The latter, however, unlike Edgar, ruled over only a part of England and never over the whole, so it is from Edgar's coronation that this great and continuing institution may be said to date.

For a thousand years the Crown has been the key to England's nationhood and has served to implant in men the habit of feeling and acting together in national matters. The great alien princes who grasped in their strong hands the Anglo-Saxon athelings' sceptre – Canute the Dane, William the Conqueror and Henry Plantagenet of Anjou – making England for a time part of a Scandinavian, then of a Norman, and then of an Angevin international consortium or empire – cumulatively strengthened it. It became natural to Englishmen, and even Anglo-Norman barons, to act with and through the Crown. For the functioning of their local institutions, the inheritance of their lands, the administration of justice and order, were all inextricably bound up with its existence. As everywhere in the Middle Ages, society in England was intensely local; men lived and thought in terms of neighbourhood. Yet, as a result of three and a half centuries of evolution, her political and legal organization became, not provincial like that of medieval France and Spain, Germany and Italy, but monarchical. The Crown was the motive-spark of public activity and the fount of honour. An English landowner thought of himself not merely as the vassal of a provincial earl, but as a liege of the King; and an English Justice not as a functionary of a provincial court, but as a guardian of the King's peace. The organization of the realm ceased to be feudal as on the Continent; it became national. From top to bottom ran this chain of royal unity. The great men who ruled the provinces were also officers of the Sovereign's household, judicial bench and feudal army. They governed the neighbourhood and they served the King. In a descending scale the same principle applied to every division of the nation: to those who operated its institutions in shire, hundred and village, the baronial honour and manor. All stood, in one capacity or another, on the rungs of a ladder, feudal or administrative, which stretched upwards to the Throne.

One great Plantagenet king established a Common Law for all England; another, his great-grandson, Edward I, a constitutional means, Parliament, for securing his people's consent for changing the law. Before his time, when the King wished to take counsel with the nation's leaders – that is, its most powerful men – or when he wished to obtain additional money from them other than the permanent feudal and traditional dues, he called his magnates together in his Magnum Concilium or Great Council. During the struggles between them and Henry II's son and grandson, John and Henry III, the Great Council acquired what was more or less a right to be consulted at not too distant intervals. That it should be so was one of the provisions, though by no means always observed, of Magna Carta; that whenever he sought to depart from the established custom on 'known law of the land', the King should take counsel, together with his officers of state, with his tenants-in-chief.

By using periodic royal Parliaments, as they came to be called, to change and state the law, Edward I – 'the English Justinian' – gave this institution the bent which was to make it, in the fullness of time, the sovereign body it now is. With its representatives drawn from the lesser landowners or knights of the shires and from the burgesses of the trading towns, as well as from the magnates and prelates, its powers developed, partly through the desire of strong rulers to secure the utmost effective popular support for their policies, partly through the subjects' growing resolve to make bad rulers conform to the law. Sovereigns like Edward I, Edward III and Henry VIII used and fostered Parliament because they were natural leaders who believed in carrying their people with them and making them active partners in their projects. Weak and arbitrary sovereigns like Edward II, Richard II and Charles I helped the advance of Parliament – or rather of that inherent partnership between Crown and Parliament which has been the key to English history – because, in uniting their people against them, they made Parliament the champion of popular

7

rights and liberties. Great monarchs gave the country unity, and less successful ones, however unconsciously, fostered national self-government.

The tragic struggle between Crown and Parliament in the seventeenth century, when a new dynasty of Scottish kings pedantically claimed a 'divine right' to overrule Parliament, caused a libertarian, yet instinctively conservative, people during the eighteenth and nineteenth centuries to reconstitute its ancient monarchy on a more stable basis. This was that hereditary sovereigns should reign but not govern, leaving their responsibilities and odium to Ministers responsible for their actions to Parliament and, though nominally appointed by the Crown, dependent on the confidence and support of the dominant Party in the House of Commons. To that constitutional conception the present royal dynasty has remained unswervingly loyal during its two and a half centuries on the throne – that is for more than a quarter of the English royal millenium.

If the political influence and prerogatives of the Crown have, during that time, little by little diminished, its prestige and popularity have immeasurably increased. The British – a people with a genius for political evolution rather than revolution – have resuscitated an ancient, and elsewhere largely discarded, institution and adapted it to the needs of a new age. Through their reluctance to change old names and forms, a conservative but essentially practical race hit on a political device which is not an anachronism, as it might seem to superficial observers, but a most effective means for preserving and strengthening a country's cohesion and stability. More perhaps than any other single factor, it has accounted for the astonishing steadiness and resilience of the nation during the present stormy century.

For the Crown is, as it has always been, the unifying principle which unites the national family. When an English sovereign succeeds to the throne he inherits, not only a title and the outward signs and trappings of sovereignty, but his or her people's love. That instinctive feeling, centering round the throne, arises from a thousand years of an unbroken monarchical heritage. How it has evolved these pages may help to show.

The Saxons

EDGAR

973—975

Edgar was born in 944, the younger son of King Edmund, and great-grandson of Alfred the Great of Wessex, who had saved England from the Norsemen. After the death of his father he was brought up, first in the court of his uncle King Edred, and later in that of his elder brother King Edwy, until in 957 the leaders of the Mercian and Northumbrian revolt made him their king. Then in 959, when Edwy died, Edgar succeeded to his title and became nominal ruler of the English kingdoms of Wessex, Mercia, Northumbria, and East Anglia. This claim had, however, to be substantiated. A large part of England was inhabited by the descendants of fierce Danish or Norse invaders, with their own laws and leaders. During his reign, through a certain amount of force and a great deal of wise administration, Edgar succeeded in achievng the pacification and unification of his heterogeneous peoples. After a revolt in 966 he gained control of the Danish areas, and retained authority there by leaving administration in the hands of trusted local leaders and not interfering with local customs so long as it did not interfere with the peace of the realm. Thus by 973 Edgar had unified and pacified his English and Danish subjects, making of them a single, peaceful nation. His coronation was visible proof of this unity.

It was at Edgar's coronation that the earliest form of the service still used at the crowning of England's kings was read by its author, the mystic saint and musician, Archbishop Dunstan. Behind the solemn rites – the royal prostration and oath, the Archbishop's consecration and anointing, the anthem 'Zadok the Priest', linking the kings of the Angles and Saxons with those of the ancient Hebrews, the investiture with sword, sceptre and rod of justice, the shout of recognition by the assembled lords – lay the idea that an anointed king and his people were a partnership under God. After that sacramental act, loyalty to the crown became a Christian obligation. The ideal of patriotism first began to take vague shape in men's minds, superseding the older conception of tribal kingship. It was this which helped to give

England in the tenth century institutions stronger than those of any Western land. Her system of taxation, of currency and coinage, of local government, of the issue of laws and charters were all in advance of those prevailing in the half-anarchical kingdoms and dukedoms of the former Frankish empire. As a result, though a country of little account at the world's edge, her wealth and prestige increased rapidly.

After the coronation there was only one other event of any note in Edgar's reign. Later in the spring he sailed with his fleet to Chester, where he met with six or eight (accounts vary) rulers of independent British kingdoms, who swore that they would be faithful to him as 'Bretwalda' of the whole island, and promised to be his allies by land and by sea. Legend has it that the king was then rowed up the river by these sub-kings, in token of his overlordship.

Edgar died two years after his coronation, in 975, at the age of thirty-one. He was buried at the Abbey of Glastonbury, and within a hundred years he was being reverenced there as a saint.

EDWARD
THE MARTYR
975—978

Edward the Martyr succeeded his father Edgar in 975 with the support of Archbishop Dunstan, in the face of an opposition which favoured his younger half-brother Aethelred. The kingdom to which he succeeded was already much changed from the primitive tribal polity his forebears had known. This was due to the unifying and stabilizing effects of his father's reign, to the pioneer achievements of his heroic ancestor, Alfred of Wessex, and to the sagacious statesmanship of Archbishop Dunstan.

The heart of England's culture was no longer Northumbria – now a wasted and depopulated province – but Wessex. Here too, as in the great northern kingdom that had welcomed St Aidan and bred St Cuthbert, Celtic blood and tradition mingled with Saxon. Even its early kings had borne names which were not Teuton, like Cerdic, Cynric, Caewlin, and Celtic place-names were intertwined mysteriously in its western shires with English: Axe and Exe, avon for river, coombe for valley. 'In Avons of the heart' Rupert Brooke wrote a thousand years later, 'her rivers run'. The greatest Wessex figure of the age was Archbishop Dunstan, who, like his earlier countryman, St Aldhelm, had been partly nursed in the tradition of Celtic Christianity. At Glastonbury, where his first work was done, legend went back far beyond the English conquest to the tiny wattle church which St Joseph of Arimathea was supposed to have built among the watermeadows for the conversion of Roman Britain. Dunstan was a mystic, feeling his way to wisdom through visions and trances; he wrestled with fiends and monsters, and heard mysterious, heavenly voices.

With its fine craftsmen and the rule of its strong kings, England was beginning to accumulate treasures: to become a rich land worth plundering as she had partly been before the Danes attacked her. Ivories and jewelled crucifixes, golden and silver candelabra, onyx vases and elaborate wood-carvings, superbly embroidered vestments, stoles and altar-cloths adorned the churches and halls and hunting-lodges of the great.

This century saw a new flowering of Anglo-Saxon art. Archbishop Dunstan himself was a craftsman and loved to fashion jewellery and cast church-bells. He loved to work, too, in the scriptoria, as he had done as a young monk; in his day the illuminators of the monastic renaissance, with their gorgeous colouring and boldly flowing margins, surpassed that of any northern European art of the time. So did the sculptors of the Winchester school who carved the Angel at Bradford-on-Avon, the Virgin and Child at Inglesham, and the wonderful Harrowing of Hell in Bristol Cathedral.

Yet all this growing polity and wealth depended in the last resort on the ability of English kings to keep good order. Three years after his accession to the throne Edward the Martyr was stabbed near Corfe by a thane of the queen mother's household. The murder of the fifteen year old king made a deep impression; 'worse deed' wrote the chronicler 'was never done among the English'. In the sinister light of what happened afterwards it probably seemed even worse in retrospect than at the time.

AETHELRED
THE REDELESS
978—1016

The long reign of Edward the Martyr's half-brother, who succeeded him, was one of the most disastrous in English history. Aethelred the Redeless – the unready or lacking in counsel – was a spoilt, petulant weakling. Incapable of running straight, his double-dealing set the great ealdormen by the ears even before he reached manhood. Under his inconstant, passionate impulses and those of his brutal favourites, England's new-found unity dissolved.

Once more, scenting weakness as vultures carrion, the Norsemen returned. The European mainland was no longer the easy prey it had been; under the challenge of repeated invasion its divided peoples had learnt to defend themselves. But the Norsemen, whose own land had so little to offer, were not yet prepared to settle down. The northern seas and islands were still full of them. Barred out of Europe, they turned once more to England. Finding from isolated raids on the coast that her people were no longer invincible, they struck in 991 at her south-eastern shires. After a hundred years of victory, the English were confident they could repel them. They received a disquieting awakening.

There was little to redeem the record of the next twenty years. Under their feckless king, who 'let all the nation's labour come to nought', nothing went right for the English. 'When the enemy is eastwards' wrote the Anglo-Saxon chronicler, 'then our forces are southward; and when they are southward, then our forces are northward . . . Anything that may be counselled never stands for a month'. The English were not only outmanoeuvred; they were betrayed. Some of the ealdormen and the feeble king's favourites threw in their lot with the enemy, shifting from side to side in selfish attempts to increase their dominions.

Only two glorious incidents stand out in the whole of this disgraceful period. The first was the Battle of Maldon where an ealdorman, Brihtnoth, with a small band of followers, opposed the Danes on the banks of the Blackwater; and the second was a heroic defence of London during which the English, with the aid of Olav of Norway, managed to pull down London Bridge from under the feet of the embattled Danes by attaching ropes to the piles which supported it and rowing away downstream with the ebb tide.

These were isolated incidents, however, in a period of otherwise unmitigated disaster. England's only respite was when Aethelred, bleeding her people white with taxes, bribed the Danes to withdraw. But as soon as they had spent the money they returned for more, harrying the country until a new ransom, or danegeld, was raised.

Lacking the strong hand they respected, the Danes of northern England turned to plundering their kinsmen. Indeed, Aethelred drove them to it, harrying their homesteads with the same barbarity as the invaders harried his own. 'He went into Cumberland' the chronicler wrote 'and ravaged it well nigh all'. His crowning act of folly occurred in 1002 when he gave orders for a massacre of the Danes living in York, among them the sister of the King of Denmark. The revenge taken by the bloodthirsty king, Sweyn Forkbeard, was as terrible as deserved. In 1013, after over ten years of ceaseless harrying by Sweyn, Aethelred fled to Normandy, leaving his desolate country in the hands of the invader. In 1014 he was allowed to return, on condition that he mended his ways. But in 1015 Sweyn's son, Canute, decided to take a hand, and made yet another attack. Before the conflict could be resolved, Aethelred died, leaving his son Edmund Ironside to continue the struggle.

EDMUND IRONSIDE

1016

When Aethelred fled ignominiously to the continent in 1013, he left behind him a very able son to carry on the fight. Edmund, the king's eldest surviving son, was to spend the remaining two years of his father's reign, and the seven months of his own, trying to uphold his own line against the Danish invader, Canute. For three years the two great soldiers, Englishman and Dane, fought each other among the forests and marshes of southern England.

In the summer of 1015 Edmund carried off and married, in defiance of his father, the widow of one of the murdered thegns of the northern Danelaw, taking possession of all their property. As a rebel against the king who had so recently laid waste so much of that country, he was assured of a welcome, and by the end of that summer he had been accepted as lord by the whole confederation of the Five Boroughs of the Danelaw.

This gave Edmund a tremendous fighting force – but not quite enough. Twice he tried to join forces with Eadric of Mercia, but was defeated by the latter's treachery. Twice he tried to rally the men of London to his support, but was foiled by their refusal to fight without the leadership of King Aethelred. So at last, in the spring of 1016, Edmund moved to London to join forces with his father. When, on St George's Day of that year Aethelred at last died, Edmund was chosen king by the men of London and magnates who had come in from the country to help defend the town.

Unfortunately, within days of Aethelred's death a more widely representative assembly met at Southampton, and swore fealty to Canute in return for a promise of good government. Six months later, after five astonishing victories on the part of the English loyalist forces – at Penselwood on the Somerset–Dorset border, at Sherston in Wiltshire, on the Western road to London, at Brentford, and at Otford in Kent – the young Edmund was himself defeated by Canute at Ashenden in Essex, through the treachery, once again, of Eadric of Mercia, that vile favourite of his father's.

'When the king learnt that the army had gone inland,' wrote the monkish scribe of the Anglo-Saxon Chronicle, 'for the fifth time he collected all the English nation; and pursued them and over-took them in Essex at the hill which is called Ashenden, and they stoutly joined battle there. Then Ealdorman Eadric did as he had often done before and was the first to start the flight . . . and thus betrayed his liege lord and all the people of England'.

A few weeks later, after signing a pact with Canute near Deerhurst on the Severn, by which the country was to be divided between them, Edmund died suddenly at Oxford.

The Danes

CANUTE
1016—1035

In the midwinter of disaster that culminated in the death of young King Edmund, the great Council or Witan met and made its terms with the Danish conqueror. Preferring strength on the throne to weakness, and unity to division, it elected as king not one of Edmund's infant sons, but the young Dane, Canute. It proved a wise choice. For though Canute was almost as ruthless as his father, he ended the long scourge of Norse invasions. At a meeting of the Witan in Oxford he swore to govern his new realm by the laws of King Edgar. Henceforward he made no distinction between his new countrymen and his old.

For if Canute had conquered England, in a wider sense England conquered him. English missionaries, following Boniface's great tradition, had long been at work in Scandinavia; though born a pagan, Canute had himself been baptized. With his acceptance of a Christian crown the ravaging of Christendom from the north ceased. While in many things still a heathen, revengeful and hard, he became a devout churchman, enforcing tithes, endowing monasteries, and even making a pilgrimage to Rome where he laid English tribute on the altar of St Peter. A poem of the time describes his visit to a Fenland abbey:

> Merry sungen the monkes in Ely
> When Cnut King rowed thereby.
> 'Row, cnichts, near the land,
> And hear we these monkes sing.'

Part of Canute's political policy was to establish the four major earldoms of Northumbria, East Anglia, Mercia, and Wessex as centres of power. In the long term, however, this was to prove disastrous. For the rivalry between them, under the weak, pious Edward the Confessor, was to lead ultimately to the break-up of the state, the successful invasion by William of Normandy and the end of the Anglo-Saxon line.

The famous legend about Canute illustrates his strong, realist character and the esteem in which his people held him. It is probably apocryphal, but shows the persistence of his reputation as a wise and good king. It was said that his courtiers sought to please him by flattery in assuring him that his power was so great that, if he commanded the tide not to rise, the waves would obey him. To show them their folly, Canute bade them carry his chair to the edge of the sea, where he sat and waited until the tide rose round his ankles.

Had this great, though harsh, man lived, the course of European history might have been different. Being king of both England and Denmark, he tried to make the North Sea an Anglo-Danish lake and England the head of a Nordic confederation stretching from Ireland to the Baltic. After his conquest of Norway he became virtual emperor of the North. But fate was against him. He died at forty in 1035, his work incomplete and most of his mighty projects still a dream. He was buried at Winchester among the English kings, while his half-barbaric Danish sons divided his Scandinavian empire between them.

HAROLD HAREFOOT

1035—1040

The period following Canute's death was a miserable anticlimax
to a reign which, though imposed by conquest, had given England
comparative peace for nearly twenty years. His sons proved
incapable of maintaining his position of dignity and power,
and there was no stability in the rule of either. The empire which
the great Dane had created from the union of his Scandinavian
conquests with his English kingdom had been showing signs of
disintegration even before his death. Yet his position in England
itself had never been stronger than at the end of his reign. Within
seven years the inept rule of his sons had destroyed all hope of a
continued union of the northern peoples. That England herself
managed to weather the storm was due only to the strength of her
institutions and to their recovery during the long period of peace
and order under Canute, and also to the merciful briefness of his
sons' reigns.

When Canute died in 1035 his one indisputably legitimate son,
Hardicanute, was already established as ruler of the kingdom of
Denmark. But owing to a growing threat to that kingdom from
Norway, it was impossible for him to leave Denmark and lay
claim to his English inheritance. This faced the dead king's
Danish and English counsellors in England – responsible for
deciding the succession – with a dilemma. Was it better to take
the risks involved in having an absentee ruler in order to maintain
the hereditary principle? Or was it better to by-pass the direct
bloodline, and select a ruler whose presence could ensure stability?

The crisis found them divided in opinion. One party, headed
by Queen Emma and Earl Godwine of Wessex, favoured the former
solution and declared for Hardicanute. The other, supported by
Earl Leofric of Mercia and the sea-traders of London, was un-
willing to make any final decision, and proposed what was then
a novel idea, a regency. Their proposed candidate was Harold,
known as Harefoot, an illegitimate son of Canute by one of his
mistresses. At a council held at Oxford he was elected regent, to

rule in his brother's place until such time as Hardicanute could occupy the throne himself.

The experiment ended in failure, as it was bound to do in that rough age when a ruler needed the authority of full and recognized kingship to survive at all. Unsatisfied with the throne alone, Harold set out to win, by fair means or foul, the crown. His first act was to lay hands on the treasury and to 'expel from England, without pity at the beginning of winter', Queen Emma, mother of Hardicanute and the chief champion and protector of the latter's rights. But having achieved the crown that he was so intent on wresting from his brother, he showed little sign of being able to hold it against an invasion planned by Hardicanute and his mother, the exiled Queen Emma. Before, however, the invaders, sailing from Bruges in Flanders, could arrive to wreak their vengeance on the usurper and recover the kingdom, Harold died at Oxford on 17 March 1040.

HARDICANUTE

1040—1042

When, having made a settlement with his troublesome neighbour, King Magnus of Norway, and assembled a fleet to invade England, the legitimate Danish claimant to the throne of England, Hardicanute, at long last landed on her soil at the invitation of his bastard half-brother's former subjects, his first act was to order the corpse of the dead usurper to be dug up and flung into a marsh and, later, into the Thames, with every accompaniment of ignominy. His next was to levy an exorbitant tax to pay for his invasion fleet. Neither tended to make him popular. Nor, when two of his house-carls, while levying the tax, were murdered by the mob at Worcester, did his subsequent burning of that city and the harrying of the Worcestershire countryside.

For Hardicanute appeared to have inherited all his father's failings and none of his virtues. He was brutal, treacherous, malicious and violent. He even betrayed one of his English earls when under a pledge of protection – a particularly horrid deed in the eyes of a primitive rustic people. The only good thing recorded of him was that he was kind to his half-brothers, the sons of his mother, Emma of Normandy, by her marriage to Aethelred the Redeless. And it was by the eldest of these dispossessed athelings of the old Anglo-Saxon royal line, the forty-year-old Edward – whom he made a member of his household and even appointed as his heir – that he was succeeded when, still in his middle twenties, he was taken ill at the marriage feast of one of his Danish retainers, dying suddenly, on 8 June 1042, 'as he stood at his drink'.

So Canute's abortive North Sea empire perished with his sons, and England's throne returned to her native dynasty. In the same way two centuries earlier Charlemagne's far larger continental empire had dissolved when his strong hand was removed. Barbarian kings, unless they were men of the most exceptional calibre, could not govern large areas. They lacked roads and bridges, trained public servants, the means of regular administration and justice. They thought of their dominions as family possessions

25

which they were free to dispose of as they pleased. Even when they ruled, like Canute, with a sense of vocation, they could not transmit it to their sons who, by tribal and family custom, had the right to divide their patrimony. They could not give their peoples the continuity and security from which spring patriotism and the habit of subordinating self to the public interest.

EDWARD THE CONFESSOR

1042—1066

'In this year' (1043), ran the account in the monastic Anglo-Saxon Chronicle, 'Edward was consecrated as king at Winchester on Easter Sunday with great ceremony . . . Archbishop Eadsige consecrated him and gave him good instruction before all the people, and admonished him well for his own sake and for the sake of all the people.' Edward, son of Aethelred the Redeless by his second wife, Emma of Normandy, was a soft, devout, peace-loving man. Though exile in his mother's country had made him more French than English, his subjects were much impressed by his piety. He was more like an abbot than a king; the Confessor they called him. His greatest interest was in the building of a monastery among the river marshes at Thorney, a mile or two to the west of London. Here, that he might watch his abbey rising – the West Minster, as it was called – he made himself a small palace that was one day to become the heart of an Empire.

Yet Edward exposed his subjects to almost as many dangers as his father, the Redeless. He was so devout that he refused to give his wife a child and his realm an heir. Absorbed in works of piety he left its affairs to the great ealdormen and his Norman favourites. Edward had inherited a court made up almost entirely of Anglo-Danish warriors and statesmen, the remnant of another age and another line. It was not surprising, under the circumstances, that he turned for support to men from the country in which he had spent his childhood, and with whom he felt at home. He surrounded himself with French-speaking Norman knights and clergymen, and his patronage of them greatly offended his English subjects. In order to pacify the latter he made large grants of royal land to the most troublesome of their magnates, particularly to Godwine, Earl of the West Saxons. This able, but ruthless and ambitious, man induced the king to marry his daughter and to confer on his spoilt, quarrelling sons the earldoms of East Anglia, Glouces-ter, Hereford, Oxford, Northampton, Huntingdon, and Northern

Northumbria. The jealousies aroused by his greatness and the crimes of his eldest son led at one time to his temporary eclipse and banishment. But he returned to England at the head of a fleet, harried its coasts and, with the help of the Londoners, dictated terms to the throne.

The chaotic power of the English ealdormen was not entirely Edward's fault. It was also the result of a cumulative alienation of royal estates – caused by the difficulty of raising revenue to pay for public services – which had been going on for generations, and which had increasingly deprived the monarchy of its chief and, in that age of primitive organization and communications, almost only regular source of income.

Yet compared with those of his predecessors and successors, Edward's long reign was mainly uneventful. Except for the usual harrying of the borders by the Scots and Welsh and of the sea-coasts by Danish pirates, and despite the turbulence of the greater magnates, he was left in comparative peace, to build his abbey and to live a life more monastic than regal. His was a reign, therefore, to which his subjects were to look back in the future with considerable nostalgia.

On 5 January 1066, a few days after the consecration of his abbey church at Westminster, the gentle Confessor died and was buried in the Minster he had built.

HAROLD

1066

When the Confessor died there were three hereditary claimants to the English throne – his great-nephew, William Duke of Normandy; Harold Hardrada, King of Norway; and a son of Edmund Ironside. But the Witan, meeting in the Godwine stronghold of London, ignored them all and elected Harold Godwinson, Earl of Wessex – son of the great Earl Godwine and brother to the queen. And this notwithstanding the fact that Harold, when shipwrecked in Normandy, had earlier done homage to William and sworn to assist his claim.

All that summer of 1066 two armadas were preparing to invade England, one on the Norman coast, the other in the Norwegian fiords and islands to the north of Scotland. But though Harold, concentrating against the nearer of the two, waited all summer in the south, by the autumn his peasant levies began to slip away to their homes and harvests. Only the house-carls of the royal bodyguard remained, until, in September, news came that the King of Norway had landed in the Ouse, near York.

Harold at once set out on the long march up the straight, grass-grown military high-road which the Romans had built a thousand years before. Four years earlier the lightning speed of his marches had broken the power of the Welsh. Now he was resolved that the Viking king who had come to seize his kingdom should meet the same end, promising him six feet of English earth or, as he was tall, seven. On 25 September, after covering thirty miles since dawn, he fell on the Viking host at Stamford Bridge. All afternoon the clangour of axe and sword continued. By dusk Hardrada had fallen, and King Harold – 'a little man sitting proudly in his stirrups' – had made good his boast that his foe should win nothing in England but a grave.

Two days later, William, who had been waiting for a favouring wind, sailed from the Somme. On 28 September he landed in Pevensey Bay. The news, galloped through the Midland forests, took two days to reach York where Harold was celebrating his victory. Without a moment's hesitation he and his battered house-carls set out again for the south. In six days they covered the 190 miles to London. Waiting there a few days for the fyrd of the southern shires to join them, they marched on 12 October for Hastings. Uncertain of his kingdom's loyalty and fearful lest his jealous earls should play him false, Harold had to burn out the southern wasps' nest like the northern or perish.

The battle which was to decide his fate and England's took place on 14 October at Senlac where the Hastings track emerged from the Sussex oak-forest. The English king, who had meant to attack, was forced to remain on the defensive, as only half his troops had arrived. His house-carls, with their double-handed battle-axes, were probably the finest infantry in Europe, but the rest of his army was a rabble of peasant levies, armed with spears, clubs and pitchforks, and no match for Duke William's armoured knights. Fighting continued all day, but by the evening only the house-carls were left holding the ridge against the Norman horsemen. They were so closely packed that the fallen had scarcely room to fall. It was almost dark when a band of knights closed in on Harold who had been wounded in the eye by an arrow, and, as he bent bleeding over his shield, hacked him in pieces. 'In the English ranks', wrote a Norman chronicler, 'the only movement was the dropping of the dead. They were ever ready with their steel, those sons of the old Saxon race, the most dauntless of men'. By nightfall all lay dead round their fallen king and his banner of the Fighting Man.

The Normans

WILLIAM
THE CONQUEROR

1066—1087

William, Duke of Normandy and Conqueror of England, was one of the great men of history. His mother was the unmarried daughter of a Falaise tanner; his great-great-grandfather had been a Viking pirate. Left fatherless as a child, his boyhood had been spent amid the turmoil caused by the violence of his father's feudal barons. The ruin their anarchic quarrels and indiscipline unloosed left an indelible impression on him. Of indomitable will and courage, he soon proved himself their equal in battle. As a statesman he was the master of every sovereign of the age. Far-sighted, patient, prudent, self-controlled, bold but thorough in all he did, and ruthless towards those who stood in his way, he made his little duchy, with its disciplined chivalry of armoured knights and ruddy-faced men-at-arms from the Normandy apple-orchards, the most formidable force in Europe. Compelled to wage war in turn against his own barons, his jealous neigh-bours in Maine, Anjou and Brittany, and his feudal overlord, the titular king of France, he defeated them all. He never lost sight of his aims, never over-reached himself and steadily increased his domains.

In 1066, on the Confessor's death, he claimed the throne of England which its Witan had conferred on the warrior ealdorman, Harold Godwinson. Landing in Pevensey Bay that autumn he routed Harold in the battle of Hastings and was crowned on Christmas Day in the Confessor's new abbey at Westminster. With a few thousand knights and men-at-arms he had conquered a nation of nearly two millions.

During the next generation, seizing on every act of disobedience or rebellion, he transferred the ownership of every large estate from English hands to Norman. But by making not only his tenants-in-chief but all large land-holders swear to obey him even against their own overlords, he made them directly respon-sible to the Crown as in no other land in Europe. He thus restored to England what she had lacked since the days of Edgar and Canute – an effective central power.

William was hard and ruthless: 'so stark a man', an English monk called him. Above all, he was a merciless taxer. His first act after his coronation was to 'lay on a geld exceeding stiff'. Close-fisted and grasping he compiled at the end of his reign, that he might tax his realm more closely, a record of all feudal holdings directly liable to the Crown. 'So narrowly did he cause the survey to be made', wrote an English chronicler 'that there was not one single hide nor rood of land, nor – it is shameful to tell, but he thought it no shame to do – was there an ox, cow or swine that was not set down in the writ'. Using commissioners to hold local enquiries or inquests in every shire and hundred, he had recorded, with meticulous efficiency, the ownership and taxable value of every manor or village under lordship, both at the Conquest and at the time of the survey. This included the number of its hides or ploughlands, of the freemen, villeins, cottars and slaves living on it, of its mills, fish-ponds and plough-teams, the extent of its woodland, meadow and pasture – everything that was capable of being taxed. Drawn up on long parchment rolls, the survey was copied into two volumes christened by the English 'Domesday' because there was no appeal against it. It was the most remarkable administrative document of the age.

The taxation William imposed fell directly on the rich, but, as the rich could pass it on, even more on the poor. Yet the Norman Conquest brought compensations to the underdog. For William conquered more than the English. He used the heritage and administration of the athelings to curb his Norman nobility. He brought feudalism under royal control. He made England a disciplined land, disciplined not only at the base but at the summit.

WILLIAM RUFUS
1087—1100

It was England's good fortune that during the first three centuries after the Norman conquest so many of her rulers possessed kingly qualities. William the Conqueror himself had tremendous presence. 'He was of such strength of arm', wrote the historian, William of Malmesbury, 'that no one could bend the bow which he drew when his horse was at full gallop. His dignity was of the highest, despite the deformity of a protruding stomach'. It was because his able, tough, short-set second son, William, had character too that the Conqueror on his death-bed in 1087 sent his English crown, sword and sceptre to him instead of to his weak, good-natured eldest son, Robert of Normandy.

Rufus, or the Red King as William II was called from his flaming hair, was a bad man – reckless, vicious, illiterate, cruel and blasphemous. But his English subjects, shocked though they were by his life, remembered with gratitude 'the good peace he kept in the land'. 'He was very strong and fierce to his country', wrote one of them, 'and to all his neighbours and very terrible'. He feared, it was said, God little and man not at all.

When the Norman barons, who turned his elder brother Duke Robert's, duchy into an inferno, raised trouble in England they got short shrift. Rufus had his cousin, who was one of them, whipped in every church in Salisbury and hanged. And when he needed help against his rich French-speaking subjects, he did not hesitate to arm his weaker English-speaking ones against them: his 'brave and honourable English', he called them. Seeing in him the defender of the good order which enabled them to cultivate their fields in peace, they turned out for him with a will.

William's brief reign is chiefly remembered for two things. One was his building of the first Westminster Hall as the banquetting hall of the new royal palace of Westminster which, adjoining the Confessor's abbey and two miles from the great trading city of London, was increasingly taking the place of the old capital of Wessex, Winchester, as the heart of the nation's administration. The other was his bitter quarrel over the question of ecclesiastical investitures with the all-powerful Church, whose bishoprics, in defiance of papal displeasure, he conferred on evil-living favourites and whose English metropolitan see, Canterbury, he kept vacant for four years after the death of his father's primate, Lanfranc, in order to enjoy its revenues. In 1093, when he fell desperately ill, in abject terror of eternal hell-fire he hastily conferred the see on the saintly scholar and philosopher Anselm, Abbot of Bec. But after the vicious king's recovery the new Archbishop, sooner than compromise the Church's rights, went into voluntary exile, and the quarrel was only resolved by William's death from an assassin's arrow while hunting in the New Forest – the great royal pleasure-preserve which the Conqueror, 'who loved the tall deer like a father', had enclosed.

HENRY I

1100—1135

William Rufus was succeeded on the throne of England by his younger brother, Henry, the Conqueror's youngest son. It was largely his English subjects who later enabled him to wrest Normandy also from his elder brother, Duke Robert. At the battle of Tinchebrai, forty years after Hastings, English infantry, fighting side by side with Anglo-Norman knights, overthrew the baronage of the Duchy. They were trained by the king himself who taught them how to resist cavalry. Though he was as grasping as his father, the English – whose despised tongue he learnt to speak – made a hero of Henry who, unlike his brothers, had been born in their land. His title to the throne being uncertain, he proclaimed his adherence to English law, swore in his coronation oath to maintain justice and mercy, and promised to 'abolish all the evil practices with which the realm was unjustly oppressed'. He claimed that he had been called to the throne in the Anglo-Saxon electoral way, 'by common counsel of the barons of the realm'. Soon after his accession he married a daughter of the Scots king, who through her English mother was descended from Edmund Ironside, Edgar and Alfred.

Henry I, 'the Lion of Justice', as he was called, deserved his people's confidence. 'There was great awe of him', testified the Anglo-Saxon chronicler, 'no man durst misdo against another in his time; he made peace for man and beast'. For thirty-five years this squat, avaricious, smooth-spoken man gave England that political stability which those who have known anarchy most value. He was a tremendous worker, a man of business who could read Latin, understood the importance of administration, and introduced into government regular habits and routine. His father had given England a taxing system more accurate and honest than any in Europe; building on his foundations Henry gave it a permanent officialdom. He made it out of the domestic officers of his household – the Treasurer, the Chamberlain who looked after the bedchamber, the Constable of the knights, and the Marshal of the stables, the Steward who presided in the hall where scores of ushers kept order with rods, the revered Chancellor with his seal and writing-office where writs were prepared for the sheriffs.

The greatest of the royal servants was the Justiciar, who kept order when the king sat in judgement and deputized for him in his absence. He and his fellow officers formed a kind of inner standing court of the Great Council known as the Curia Regis, to which both judicial appeals and affairs of state were referred. With their staffs of trained clerks, and their chambers where suitors could wait on them, they were the first fathers of our Civil Service. In the great new stone hall of Westminster business continued even when the Court was travelling. Here twice a year, under the chairmanship of king or Justiciar, officials called Barons of the Exchequer sat at a table with counters and a chequered cloth, carefully checking with the sheriffs the taxes, rents, fines and debts due to the Crown. Every penny had to be accounted for. There was nothing else like it at the time in western Europe.

This capacity for organization, for creating continuing institutions, made a deep impression on Henry's contemporaries. They admired the unhurried regularity and dignity with which he did business: his daily reception before the midday meal of all who came for justice, the carefully planned arrangements for state progresses through his dominions. His influence was felt in every county where the sheriffs were kept perpetually busy, receiving writs, making records and collecting the revenues under the eyes of the royal officers at Westminster.

STEPHEN

1135—1154

After Henry I's death in 1135 from a surfeit of hunting and lampreys, Englishmen had an experience, for the first time since the Conquest, of living under a weak king. His only legitimate son having been drowned crossing the Channel, Henry had nominated as successor his daughter, Matilda, wife of the Count of Anjou, Geoffrey Plantagenet – so called from the sprig of broom he wore in his helmet. But the Council, deeming a woman unfit to rule and exercising the old English right of election from the royal house, offered the crown instead to Henry's nephew, Stephen of Blois, son of the Conqueror's daughter. This good-natured monarch lacked the qualities for kingship. 'A mild man, soft and good, and did not justice', an English chronicler wrote of him; 'he began many things but never finished them'. Though he reigned for nineteen years – 'nineteen long winters', the chronicler called them – he left little behind him save a chapel at Westminster bearing his name and an abiding memory of the anarchy unloosed by his weakness. Taking advantage of his indecision, the Welsh descended from their mountains to sack farms on the Dee and Wye, and a savage horde from Scotland marched into England, massacring the inhabitants and driving off the women and children, roped naked together, as slaves.

In 1139 Matilda, too, invaded the country from Anjou. For eight years England was racked by civil war, while local barons, playing their own selfish game, threw in their lot, first with one side, then with another. Freed from the control of the Curia Regis, the worst of them built castles from which they plundered their neighbours and indulged in all the licence – so familiar on the Continent but now almost forgotten in England – of private war. Some, like King Stephen himself, brought murderous foreign mercenaries into the country and turned the royal fortresses, of which they were custodians, into private strongholds. 'They put men in prison for their gold and silver, they hung them up by the feet and smoked them with foul smoke ... They put knotted strings round their heads and writhed them until they went into

39

the brain. They put them into dungeons crawling with adders and snakes . . . Men said that Christ and his Saints slept.' The fields were untilled, the crops destroyed, the cattle driven away. Elsewhere such doings were normal. In England, after seventy years of strong rule and royal justice, they were not.

In the end the anarchy was ended by a compromise. It was agreed that Stephen should reign till his death and be succeeded by Matilda's twenty-year-old son, Henry Plantagenet, now Count of Anjou. In 1153 Henry came to England and, amid tumultuous rejoicing, was accepted by Stephen as his 'son' and heir. When a year later, on the king's death, he was crowned and invested at Westminster with the regalia of England – golden crown and sceptre, silver-gilt rod and spurs, embroidered sandals and mantle of white silk – every bell in London rang for joy.

The Plantagenets

HENRY II

1154—1189

At twenty-one Henry II was the richest prince in Europe. He was ruler not only of England and Anjou, but of Maine, Touraine and Normandy. His marriage with Eleanor of Aquitaine – the greatest heiress of the age – made him master of south-western France. He was well-read, eloquent, courteous, and as at home in the camp as in court.

At the core of his being lay a demonic energy. He was always moving, always active. He rose before cockcrow and, slaving far into the night on public business, only sat down to ride or eat. He never wasted, or brooked a minute's delay.

As soon as he ascended the throne this restless genius began, with furious energy, to restore his kingdom. He sent away the foreign mercenaries, dismantled the unlicensed castles and demanded back the filched Crown lands. Dominion had come to him so early that conquest made no appeal to him. What he wanted was to make his rule endure. The supreme object of his crowded stormy life was to create institutions which would preserve his inheritance after his death. The means he used was law.

At the time of his accession there were five different systems of law in England, only one of them royal. Henry first sought control of the Shire and Hundred courts. He revived his grandfather's practice of sending out Exchequer barons *in itinere* to enforce his fiscal rights. Gradually he created a body of trained judges whose business it was 'to do justice habitually'. They were assigned to regular circuits of counties round which, escorted by sheriffs and javelin men, they rode on annual progresses. Others, sitting on a marble bench in Westminster Hall, formed a permanent judicial tribunal of the *Curia Regis* which grew into the courts of King's Bench and Common Pleas.

Appealing to native English tradition and under guise of restoring 'the good old laws', Henry used the prerogative to bring the whole system of freehold tenure under his law. By making the smaller landowner's right to his property dependent on the royal, instead of the feudal, courts, he struck at the root of the great lord's power over his military tenants. And he dealt a death blow to trial-by-battle and private war. Selfish, crafty, unscrupulous, the great lawyer king wielded the sword of justice 'for the punishment of evil-doers and the maintenance of peace and quiet for honest men'. His judges made his remedies available in every corner of the realm. With the precedents they enshrined in their judgments they created a Common Law for all England.

By the end of Henry's reign there was no major offence against the public peace which could not bring the offender within range of a royal writ. By making the Common Law the permanent embodiment of a righteous king sitting in judgment, the great Angevin established the English habit of obedience to law, which has been the key to the nation's peaceful continuity and progress.

Yet in trying to subject every part of his kingdom's life to the law, Henry fell foul of the one Power which in that age no ruler could safely defy – the Church. By doing so he suffered a defeat which impressed his contemporaries more than all his triumphs. The man who inflicted it was the worldly favourite he had made Archbishop of Canterbury in order to bring the Church's criminal jurisdiction under royal control. It was Thomas Becket's unexpected and spectacular championship of the Church's rights which, after eight years of bitter confrontation, provoked the enraged king's passionate outburst and the sacrilegious murder of the defiant archbishop on the steps of his own cathedral. For à Becket martyrdom resulted in his elevation to sainthood and a permanent place in the national Valhalla, and, for a penitent Henry, abasement at the feet of the scourging Canterbury monks.

RICHARD I

1189—1199

Henry II's last years were embittered by the rebellions of his sons. His eldest having died before him, he was succeeded by the thirty-two-year-old Richard 'Coeur de Lion', a giant, golden-haired warrior whose one ambition was to join the Third Crusade to recover the Christian kingdom of Jerusalem, the news of whose capture by the Saracens had shocked western Europe in the year before his accession. This chivalrous, romantic young knight, poet and musician, was so eager to raise an army that he declared he would sell anything, even London, to do so.

Though he turned his back on his kingdom and sailed away into the Orient, he proved a magnificent leader. Despite the fiery temper which made enemies of all his fellow sovereigns, he was the hero of the Crusade and put new heart into the dispirited, plague-ridden army besieging Acre. The zeal with which, stricken with fever, he pressed home the attack, led to the city's early fall. Two months later, by his great victory at Arsuf, he opened the road to Jaffa and Jerusalem. And though the final prize eluded him, and he was forced to return with his work incomplete, he made a treaty with the Saracens which for another half-century secured the beleaguered Christian kingdom of the Levant and the pilgrims' road to the Holy Places. He made the name of the northern land over which he ruled more honoured than it had ever been before. Even Saladin praised him. And though hated by crafty and intriguing princes he was loved by simple fighting men for his lion heart, his constancy to his word and his frank open nature and generosity. His shield of golden lions and scarlet crusader's cross became part of the heritage of England.

Yet the chief effect of his crusade on his subjects was the amount they had to pay to support it. The drain on their purses did not even end with the cost of equipping his fleets and armies. For when, after three years' absence, he was shipwrecked on his way home and captured by one of the many Continental princes with whom he had quarrelled, they were called upon to pay the greatest tax in their history for his ransom. It was testimony to the hold the monarchy had taken on their hearts that they paid it willingly. It was a sign of their growing wealth that they were able to pay it at all.

What was even more remarkable was that the anarchy which had divided England under Stephen and before the Conquest did not recur during Richard's absence. The permanent officials and judges Henry II had trained and the institutions he had created continued to ensure justice and order. Indeed – and this was the test of the dead king's statesmanship – the nation continued to grow in cohesion and wealth even under a sovereign who neglected his business. For Englishmen, set on the true course of their national development by the great Angevin, were learning to govern themselves.

JOHN
1199—1216

When Richard met his death besieging a Limousin castle he was succeeded by his brother, John, Henry II's youngest son. This tough, sallow, moody, highly intelligent little man – he was only 5 feet 5 inches high – had much of his father's energy and genius for administration. But, having been spoilt in childhood by both parents – who, though they quarrelled bitterly, doted on this precocious and entertaining child of their middle age – he could never discipline himself and, though a ruthless tyrant when his passions were roused, was unable to discipline others. A sustained course of action was beyond him. His ever-changing, unpredictable moods made him, sooner or later, everyone's enemy.

John could never rid himself of a suspicion that everyone was trying to defraud him, or of a habit of grabbing whatever he could. He rarely trusted any man or missed a chance of cheating one. With his sly, vulpine face, slanting eyes and deceptive geniality and charm, he grew up without morals or sense of responsibility. Sensual and grossly self-indulgent, with a passion for jewels and rich garments, he could be both munificent and absurdly mean. He owned a library of theological books and was exceptionally clean in his person, once taking as many as eight baths in a half a year. Yet he loved nothing better than watching prisoners being tortured in filthy dungeons.

To these traits he added the wild temper of his race. He suffered from maniacal rages when his body became so contorted as to be unrecognizable, when his eyes flashed fire and his dark, sallow face turned livid, as he rolled on the floor, gnawing the rushes. Intensely jealous and suspicious, he intrigued against his ministers and took pride in lying and breaking faith. Often successful in the short run – for he was capable of great, though unsustained, resolution – his ventures never ended well.

He began by losing most of the Angevin empire. In three years he lost to the King of France everything north of the Loire. Having suffered a humiliating defeat in a Continental war, he involved himself in a struggle with the Pope over the latter's appointment to the see of Canterbury of the most distinguished English scholar and churchman of the day, Stephen Langton. By doing so he involved his country in the horrors of a five years' Interdict under which the churches were closed and the church-bells silenced – a terrible deprivation for a medieval people. Finally, after making an abject surrender at the feet of a Papal Legate, yielding his kingdom as a feudatory of the Church, he entered into bitter quarrels with his baronage to whom his tyrannical and lawless exactions had become so intolerable that they took up arms and, in a dramatic confrontation in the Runnymede water-meadows on 15 June 1215, made him subscribe to a Charter binding him to govern by law. Under it he swore never again to levy new taxes on his tenants without consent of his Great Council; that heirs should be admitted to their inherit-tances and their estates not wasted during their infancies; that the merchant's stock, craftsman's tools and peasant's wainage should be free from amercement. 'To none', he had to swear, 'will we sell, to none deny or delay right or justice'.

Called Magna Carta because of its length, though its chief beneficiaries were royal tenants-in-chief, it was a national as well as feudal document. It established a precedent of immense significance for the future: that, when a king broke the feudal compact and so gave his tenants the right to renounce their allegiance, it was not necessary to dissolve the bonds of political society and disintegrate the realm. By giving the Council power to enforce the Law even against the King, Magna Carta was a constitutional expedient to enforce customary Law without revolution.

HENRY III

1216—1272

John did not keep his compact, and, in a war against the barons in which two contending foreign and mercenary armies ravaged the country, perished at the age of forty-eight. He was succeeded by his nine-year-old son, Henry, in whose name the barons, rallying to the hereditary throne, drove out the French and Scottish invaders and re-enacted Magna Carta. Yet, though at first the little golden-haired Plantagenet seemed to embody the just laws and good peace his forebears had given England, the constitutional problems which had bedevilled his father's reign still remained.

For, though Henry III took pride in being an Englishman and christened his eldest son and heir after Edward the Confessor, he was easily swayed by those he loved, particularly the relations of his Poitevin mother and Provençal wife. As was natural in a king whose father had been forcibly constrained by his own barons, he wanted to be master in his own house. Though he pledged himself to abide by the Charter, he conceived kingship as something to be exercised, not in consultation with the 'lawful men' of his realm, but by himself alone. Holding his throne as a fief from the papal Curia, he had a particularly exalted view of a king's sacred function. This and his perennial need of money to finance the continental adventures in which, at the instigation of his Poitevin relations and the Pope, he engaged, brought him into repeated conflict with his barons who much resented his dependence on foreign favourites. For though Henry was full of splendid projects, he seldom related them to reality. He was without any capacity for understanding those who thought differently from himself. He had the narrow-mindedness of a boy and could never see a problem from any viewpoint but his own. In dealing with opponents he was quite unscrupulous; feeling, as an anointed king, that his intentions justified every subterfuge, he never attempted to keep faith with them. But as he was seldom strong enough to pursue a consistent policy, he inspired more contempt than fear.

In the later part of his reign he became embroiled with a powerful baronial and popular faction under a dynamic leader and reformer, Simon de Montfort, Earl of Leicester, who sought to curb his vagaries and expenditure by substituting for royal government the rule of a Council of fifteen magnates backed by a periodic national representative assembly or Parliament. In 1264 Henry was defeated and captured by de Montfort in a battle near Lewes. But de Montfort's experiment in government lasted only a year, and in a further battle at Evesham he was slain and the king rescued by his son and heir, the Lord Edward, who, during the last years of the reign, ruled for him.

Henry's real bent was religious, not political. He was the greatest patron of ecclesiastical architecture England has ever known. His supreme achievement was the rebuilding of Edward the Confessor's Westminster Abbey which he partly modelled on the exquisite Sainte Chapelle of his cousin, the great French king, Saint Louis. His reign, too, saw the coming to England of the first friars, who, instead of withdrawing into a life of religious contemplation like the monks, made the world their parish and the street their cloister. The all-embracing charity, cheerfulness, courtesy and example of these humble evangelists – particularly of the grey-gowned, bare-footed Franciscans – made a deep impression. Renouncing all wealth, they made their habitations in the strongholds of poverty, vice and misery. Their diocese was the lazar-house door, the stews, the stinking hovels along the stagnant ditches outside the town walls; their pulpit the dung-hill and garbage pit, the pothouse and brothel.

EDWARD I

1272—1307

When his father died Edward I was on crusade in the Holy Land, where he had been commanding the army of Christendom against the Saracens. Towering above his fellows and famous for his feats at jousting, hunting and hawking, he was the beau idéal of a medieval king, with perfect health and the vitality and good humour which sprang from it. For all his imperious will there was something noble and magnanimous about him. His harsh early experience of civil war had taught him to understand the point of view of others and to be patient and conciliatory. He knew, as his father had never known, how to work with men of different opinions. In these gentler traits, so at variance with his fierce Plantagenet temper, Edward was helped by an ideal marriage. His love for his Spanish wife, Eleanor of Castile, whose calm Gothic features still look down from her carved head in the Abbey, was the guiding star of his life. Their court was an orderly and decorous place, free from vice and grossness.

This great king, to secure support for his far-reaching legal and administrative reforms, adopted the classic dictum that 'that which touches all should be approved by all'. It was his Parliament of 1275 – far more than the rebel de Montfort's illegal one of ten years earlier – which deserves to rank as the first great English Parliament. To it he summoned, not only the magnates, the earls, barons, bishops and abbots who were his tenants-in-chief, but, through his sheriffs, four elected and representative knights from the shire-courts of every county, and four merchant burgesses from the borough court of every chartered town. By using such royal Parliaments to change and state the law Edward – 'the English Justinian' – gave to the institution its strong legislative bent. From employing it to secure popular approval for his law-making, it was only a step, though a gradual one, to the revolutionary doctrine that, without the assent of Parliament, no ordinance of the king could become effective and permanent law.

By using Parliaments to change and rationalize the law

Edward not only effected far-reaching reforms – some of which, like his land laws, were to last for centuries. He also tried to unify and give lordship and law to the whole of Britain, seeking to extend the peaceful and orderly state of his English realm to the more barbarous and chaotic west and north of the island. In Wales, after two wars against its fierce but feuding tribal patriots, he succeeded, unifying English and Welsh law and building five great castles – Conway, Carnarvon, Criccieth, Harlech and Beaumaris – to hold down the former principality of Gwynedd or North Wales, whose princedom he conferred on his infant son and heir. But in Scotland he was less successful. After nearly achieving a peaceful union of the two crowns in 1290 through a marriage of his son with the last Scottish king's child heiress – who unfortunately died before it could take place – he became involved in a long, bitter struggle with the Scottish people and their patriot leaders. One of these, the guerrilla knight, William Wallace, after eight years' resistance in his northern fastnesses, was captured in 1305, tried as a traitor in Westminster Hall and hanged, drawn and quartered. But Scotland's resistance almost immediately broke out again under a new leader, Robert Bruce, an Anglo-Scottish noble whose grandfather, though possessing a presumptive claim to the Scottish royal succession, had once been Chief Justice of the English King's Bench. To Edward's unspeakable fury this daring young man had himself crowned King of Scotland. Marching north to destroy him, Edward – 'the hammer of the Scots' – died within sight of the Scottish border in his sixty-ninth year.

EDWARD II

1307—1327

Edward I had never been happy in his son and heir, who at the age of twenty-three ascended the throne. Deprived of his mother's protective love when he was five, and left to the care of a preoccupied and increasingly autocratic father, whom he resembled only in his giant stature and superb Plantagenet physique, the second Edward had grown up frivolous and emotionally unstable, with a hatred of the knightly and martial exercises of his class and an unfashionable taste for such rustic pursuits and pastimes as digging, thatching, farriery, swimming, rowing and wrestling. His chosen companions were grooms, blacksmiths, gardeners, watermen, jesters, actors and singers. Denied all share in the counsels of his father, of whose terrible rages he stood in dread, he had only one ambition; to lead his life in his own way.

When still in his teens he had conceived an inordinate love for a handsome but penniless Gascon, Piers Gaveston, who enraged the great magnates of the realm by his presumption, insolent wit and impertinent mimicry. To their fury Edward made him his chief counsellor, showering titles and honours on him regardless of the constitutional principle for which their forefathers had contended since the days of Magna Carta, that the king should govern with the counsel and assent of his 'chief men'. Forcing him to banish Gaveston, whom, on his return with his royal master's connivance, they seized and executed, they fastened on the protesting Edward a supervisory Council, called provocatively the Lords Ordainers, which tried, not very successfully, to assume many of the royal functions.

Meanwhile the Scottish war was neglected, with the result that the penniless and, at first, almost friendless Robert Bruce gradually, in the course of the next seven years, liberated almost the whole of Scotland. Bruce had all the dogged traits of Scottish character, magnified to the point of genius: courage, persistence, unshakeable loyalty to friend and unrelenting enmity to foe, tenderness to women, genial ironic humour, logical, uncompromising ruthlessness in pursuit of his purpose. Never commanding more than a few thousand men, he evaded every attempt at capture. Whenever his foes thought they had beaten him he reappeared and, in the end, inflicted on them one of the decisive defeats of history.

This was in the summer of 1314, when, after composing their quarrel, Edward and his principal lords advanced at the head of a vast feudal host to relieve Stirling Castle. Bruce's force, covering the siege, numbered little more than a quarter of its size. But his men were defending all they held dear, while the invaders, inexperienced in Scottish warfare and supposing King Robert's hopelessly outnumbered army to be at their mercy, took few precautions as, on the eve of Midsummer Day, they encamped within sight of the beleaguered castle. Next morning, 24 June, to the amazement of the English, the Scots were seen to be advancing on them in three dense 'battles' or 'schiltrons' of massed spears. For, like the great commander he was, instead of withdrawing or awaiting the invaders' attack, Bruce, using his schiltrons of pikesmen as a moving wall of steel, intended to compress the vast mass of English knights and horses into a diminishing space between the marshes of the Forth. Before his enemies could realize what was happening, he had driven them in to the one place where he could destroy them.

Edward barely escaped with his life, while most of his army perished or were made prisoner. After Hastings, Bannockburn was the greatest military disaster in English history. It ended all hope of reconquering Scotland by arms, and when, in 1329, King Robert died at Cardross on the Clyde, a reluctant England had formally recognized Scotland's right to independence. His defeated adversary had been foully murdered a year earlier in Berkeley Castle, where he had been imprisoned by his own French queen, Isabella, and her lover, Roger Mortimer, after a general rising against him in 1327 by his disgruntled subjects.

EDWARD III

1327—1377

Edward III began his long reign as a minor of fifteen in the power
of his mother's lover and father's murderer, the rapacious Marcher
baron, Roger Mortimer. Three years later, with a band of his
young friends and fellow knights, he freed himself from that
hateful and shameful tutelage by surprising and seizing the dictator in the Queen Mother's bedroom in Nottingham Castle,
whence he was hustled off to the Tower, trial by his fellow peers,
and the gallows.

At eighteen Edward became king in fact as well as name. Like
his grandfather he meant to rule. Since childhood he had seen the
fatal consequences of a breach between a sovereign and the lords
through whom so much of the administration of a feudal kingdom had to be conducted. In an age when a journey from London
to York could take a week, there could be no governing England
without its greater nobles. After the struggles of the past generation what was needed was a compromise – a reconciliation between
royal authority and the liberties of the magnates. It was the supreme merit of this conciliatory yet shrewd young king to realize
and achieve it.

Generous, impulsive, profuse in display, a laggard neither in
love nor war, with a boyish charm which won the hearts of
warriors and fair women, Edward III was the beau idéal of
chivalry and of the elaborate code of knightly conduct and man-
ners known as courtesy. To the young English nobles he seemed
a reincarnation of their legendary hero, King Arthur. It was so
that he saw himself – the crowned leader of a brotherhood of
Christian knights. Inspired by the long rambling tales of the
Arthurian legends, he built a round tower in Windsor Castle
to accommodate a round table at which he and his knights sat
and feasted after their jousts and tournaments as equals 'in fair
fellowship'. It was to do them and his patron saint, St George,
honour that in 1347 he founded an Order, consisting of himself
and twenty-six of his most renowned companions, known as the
Knights of the Blue Garter.

A year earlier he and they had won an astonishing victory over the chivalry of France. At Crécy on the night of 26-27 August 1346 an immense French host fled before an all but encircled and hopelessly outnumbered English army, after leaving 1500 lords and knights and 10,000 common soldiers dead on the battlefield. This spectacular triumph was achieved, for a loss of only forty men, through the use of a new and overwhelming weapon, the long-bow. Aiming their massed volleys of arrows, travelling with incredible velocity, at selected target areas until every man and horse within them had been killed or maimed, the king's trained archers from the Sherwood and Macclesfield forests won victory after victory against odds. Ranging every province of western France, in two dazzling years a few thousand humble Englishmen, armed with a weapon which they alone could wield, laid the chivalry of Christendom's greatest and richest nation in the dust.

Yet just as England, in the words of the St Albans chronicler, was rejoicing in 'the abundance of peace, the plenitude of goods, and the glory of the victories', she was struck down by a sudden and dreadful pestilence. Brought into Europe from the East by Genoese traders, the 'Black Death' reached England in August 1348, and in the next year carried off a third of her peoples. No one had any idea what caused the mortality: the pallor, the sudden shivering and retching, the dreaded scarlet blotches and black boils – 'God's tokens' – the delirium and unbearable agony. Recurring three times before the end of the century, the bubonic plague, spread by rat-borne fleas, halved the country's population with far-reaching consequences. One was that, though in 1356 the English archers under the king's heir, the Black Prince, won another astonishing victory at Poitiers, by the time of Edward's death in 1377 all his conquests had been lost for lack of manpower to sustain them. Perhaps the most enduring legacies of the reign were the wonderful Crécy window at Gloucester and the crowning of Salisbury's thirteenth-century cathedral with a spire which remains one of the glories of mankind.

RICHARD II
1377—1399

When on his grandfather's death, little Richard of Bordeaux – the nine-year-old son of the dead hero of Poitiers, the Black Prince – came to the throne, England was in a sad, divided and disillusioned state. The social and economic strains caused by the Black Death, the loss of all the old king's conquests during his dotage, and a well-founded belief that there was corruption, injustice and greed in the rulers of Church and State, had brought about a universal malaise. Four years after Richard's accession it resulted in a tremendous popular explosion.

It began in the early summer of 1381 with a riot by the fisher-folk of Essex against an unjust Poll Tax. Fanned by the egalitarian preaching of wandering priests and friars, it spread like wildfire through the home counties, and within a fortnight two vast armies of peasants were marching on the capital, murdering or driving into the woods their manorial lords and the royal officers and lawyers against whom their resentment was strongest. In London the gates were opened by popular sympathizers, and the young king and his lords were besieged in the Tower. The great riverside palace of the Savoy, furnished with the spoils of ravaged France and the home of the king's uncle, John of Gaunt, was burnt; public functionaries, lawyers and foreign merchants were butchered in the streets; and the whole system of law and govern-ment, built up over the centuries, seemed about to collapse. To those born to rank and authority, cowering behind their castle walls, it was almost as though the animals had rebelled.

In this crisis Richard, then fourteen, played a hero's part. Riding out after a day in which the mob had broken into the Tower and murdered the Treasurer and Archbishop of Canter-bury, and accompanied by only a handful of followers, he met the rebel host at Smithfield to hear their grievances and demands. When their insolent, half-drunken leader, Wat Tyler, ordered one of the royal retainers to be beheaded and drew his sword on another, and the Lord Mayor, striking back, mortally wounded him, it looked as though the whole royal party, and the kingdom with it, would be destroyed.

At that moment, as thousands of peasant bows were drawn, Richard rode straight up to the massed insurgents. 'Sirs', he cried, 'will you shoot your king? I will be your captain. Let him who loves me follow me!' The effect was electric, the expected flight of arrows never came, and the whole peasant host followed him into the open country, where they were disarmed and sent home.

Yet Richard's success in taming the revolution of his poorer subjects proved his undoing. The impressionable boy, who had exorcized anarchy by the mystique of kingship, never recovered from this early intoxicating experience and the belief that, as the Lord's anointed, he could impose his will on all. This tall, yellow-haired Plantagenet – 'fair as another Absalom' – with the pale womanly face, passionate stammering speech and love of beauty, pitted himself against his nobles, the tough 'over-great subjects' whose forerunners had dethroned his great-grandfather and whom his grandfather had appeased. Possessed of considerable political astuteness, he lacked the indispensable kingly quality of steadfastness; he was hasty, fickle, tactless and arbitrary. When he claimed that the laws existed only in his own breast and exiled and confiscated without trial the lands of his able and popular cousin, Henry Bolingbroke – son of John of Gaunt and holder of the great earldoms of Lancaster, Leicester, Derby and Hereford – he alarmed every man of property in the country. In 1399, at the age of thirty-two, he was forced by a general rising to resign the crown in Bolingbroke's favour, and died a few months later, a prisoner in Pontefract Castle, in all probability by violence.

The House of Lancaster

HENRY IV

1399—1413

The deposition of Richard II in favour of his cousin, Henry Bolingbroke Duke of Lancaster, temporarily undermined the conception of primogeniture in England. For whereas Edward II's deposition seventy years earlier had been followed by the succession of his son and heir, Richard's successor – though, like him, a grandson of Edward III – was not the direct heir. He was so by virtue of his own strong arm and that of his fellow magnates. For more than a century the succession remained in dispute, and no one could feel sure who the next wearer of the Crown would be.

Son of John of Gaunt by Blanche of Lancaster – the heroine of Chaucer's earliest poem, *The Book of the Duchess* – Henry IV was a shrewd, brave and much-travelled man who had spent his early manhood crusading in eastern Europe. But owing his throne to his fellow magnates, no sooner had he ascended it than they intrigued against him as they had done against his predecessor. During his first Christmas he was nearly surprised and captured by a group of Richard's supporters. In 1403, after defeating a Scottish invasion backed by France, he was faced by a formidable conspiracy of his former ally, the great northern magnate, Henry Percy Earl of Northumberland, with the Scots nobles whom the latter had captured, and a Welsh patriot leader, Owen Glendower. Despite his victory at Shrewsbury, in which Northumberland's famous warrior son, Harry Hotspur, was killed, it took Henry five years to reduce the warlike North and an insurgent Wales. In the course of doing so, he incurred much odium for the summary execution of the Archbishop of York, Richard Scrope, who, accusing him of usurpation, had thrown in his lot with the Percys.

Among Henry's many adversaries were critics of the excessive wealth, worldliness and corruption of the Church, known as 'Lollards', who derived their unorthodox views from the teaching of an Oxford scholar and theologian, John Wycliffe, and his English translation of the Latin scriptures. Henry's father, John of Gaunt, had once been a patron of Wycliffe, as had many of the gentry who coveted the Church's surplus wealth and wished to humble the pride of the great ecclesiastical 'possessioners'. But when Wycliffe extended his attacks on the institutional side of religion to its theological mysteries and, repudiating the doctrine of transubstantiation, argued that it was idolatry to pretend that Christ's body could be made out of bread and wine by the incantations of an ignorant, and possibly sinful, priest, he lost the support of his powerful patrons. For they were not prepared to incur the risk of excommunication and eternal damnation for the sake of abstract speculations which affected neither their personal lives nor their purses. Wycliffe's russet-clad evangelists, who carried his message into the fields and hedgerows, were increasingly treated as heretics and potential rebels, not only by the Church whom they sought to disendow, but by the State – a process which became accentuated after Henry IV's accession, since the Lancastrian dynasty had to buttress its dubious claim to the throne by its orthodoxy. To help the Church suppress the Lollards Henry procured from Parliament in 1401 a statute, *De Haeretico Comburendo*, which not only condemned all unlicensed preaching and the holding of views 'contrary to the faith . . . of Holy Church', but empowered the civil arm to burn any persistent or relapsed heretic condemned by a spiritual court.

Worn out by ill health and civic dissension, Henry died at the age of forty-six in the Jerusalem Chamber of Westminster Abbey, dreaming of the days of his youth when he had been a crusader and, like the knight of his protégé, Chaucer's, *Canterbury Tales*, 'had foughten for our faith at Tramassene'.

HENRY V

1413—1422

Henry of Monmouth, who succeeded his father at twenty-five, was a soldier of genius who had learnt his trade fighting Glendower's warlike Welsh. His vision was intense but narrow and backward-looking; he thought in terms of the vanished conquests in France of his great-grandfathers, Edward III and Henry of Lancaster, and of a still older ideal – for he was a devout, even fanatic, Christian – of the Crusade to free the Holy Land. He was chaste, fearless and passionate for justice – that is, for what he considered justice – and, with his long nose, high cheek-bones and clear, inflexible eyes, ruthless in enforcing his kingly rights and obedience to his will.

He inherited a doubtful title and a debt-ridden realm, divided, violent and rebellious. Within weeks of his accession he had to defend his capital from an attempt by Lollard knights to overthrow his rule. He dealt with the insurrection with inexorable resolution. Nor was he only bent on restoring the authority of the Crown at home. He intended to enforce his rights abroad, and laid claim to the vast feudal dominions enjoyed by his ancestors in France, or, in default, to the Crown of that kingdom. Fantastic though this claim was – derived through his great-great-grandmother, Edward II's French queen – he at once set his lawyers and armourers at work to prove and enforce it.

By the summer of 1415 everything was ready for his great adventure. The crown, crown jewels and the very vestments from the Chapel Royal were pawned to pay for it. On his way to embark at Southampton, Henry's life was threatened by a plot in which his own cousin was involved. Yet he refused to be deterred and sailed for Normandy with 6000 archers and 2000 knights. Laying siege to and storming Harfleur, at the beginning of October he set out, after a third of his little force had gone down with dysentery, to march to Calais, the only remaining English possession in France. On the way he was intercepted by a vast French host. With his road barred, his outnumbered men starving and the foe about to attack him at Agincourt, on the eve of St Crispin's

63

Day – 25 October – Henry seemed doomed. Yet the morrow saw the most astonishing victory in English history. Among the 7000 French dead whom the English archers destroyed were the Constable of France and three dukes, while the French Commander-in-Chief, the royal dukes of Orléans and Bourbon and hundreds of nobles and knights were taken prisoner.

Two years later Henry returned to France. This time it was no cut-and-run raid to re-temper the blunted sword and spirit of England, but a carefully planned scheme of conquest. Laying siege to every Norman city in turn, by January 1419 he had starved the capital, Rouen, into surrender. Then, having used the prestige of Agincourt to make an alliance with the greatest of the French king's vassals, the Duke of Burgundy – lord of the rich cloth-towns of Flanders, Artois and Brabant – he demanded the French Crown, and, by a treaty negotiated at Troyes in 1420, secured the hand of the King of France's daughter and the right to rule his kingdom as Regent until his own heir should succeed to the two crowns. With the English and Burgundians driving the dis-inherited Dauphin's defeated and dispirited forces beyond the Loire, and Paris in English hands, all Henry's objectives seemed achieved. Little more than a year later the great Lancastrian hero-king, still only thirty-five, was dead, worn out by dysentery and the continuous hardships of his campaigns.

HENRY VI

1422—1461

In nine years Henry V had raised his country from disunity and decrepitude to the greatest height of power and prestige she had ever known. Yet, when his infant son by Katherine of France succeeded him, the price for his achievement had still to be paid. For the English had triumphed, not because they were braver than the French but because, under a man of passionate conviction and genius, there had been a place in their polity – and armies – for men of modest birth, armed with a weapon which they alone could wield. When, however, in 1429, a peasant girl of equal conviction and genius breathed a new spirit into the defeated chivalry and manhood of France, every Frenchman felt that the war of national independence was his own cause. And, though Joan of Arc was betrayed to the English and burnt as a heretic, five years after her martyrdom the Burgundians threw in their lot with their fellow Frenchmen.

Though for eighteen more years the English struggled to retain what they had won, they were fatally handicapped by their lack of numbers and the growing inadequacy of their financial resources. They were even more fatally handicapped by the indiscipline of their soldiers. Henry V had hanged every plunderer, forbidden offences against women and monks, and even forced his troops to mix water with their wine; and such was the terror instilled by this inflexible man that he was obeyed But once his hand was withdrawn the little army of occupation made the name of England stink in every French nostril. And when, after the defeat at Castellon in 1453 of the last English forces still fighting in France, the Government, bankrupt and exhausted, accepted the *fait accompli* and made peace, it did not end the fighting. It merely transferred it to England.

For it was not only in France that the English had lost the discipline which Henry V had given them. They had lost it at home, and, with it, the unity he had restored. During the long minority of his son, the magnates, including the king's kinsmen, contended against one another and plundered the Crown. Judges and juries refused to convict the strong; elections were fought by rival lords and knights with the help of armed mobs; and those who offended the great were hunted down by gangs of murderers in the livery of their employers. 'Get you lordship', a country squire was advised, 'hereon hangs all the law and the prophets'.

Nor did matters improve after the young king came of age. He inherited his father's piety and love of the Church, but none of his ruthlessness or strength of will. A gentle, saintly, yielding creature of touching selflessness and humility, he was powerless in the hands of whoever of his relations or counsellors had access to him. Faced by the necessities and cruelties of an iron age, with all England's remaining possessions in France lost save Calais, and with his Lancastrian and Yorkist kinsmen contending, first for the administration of the realm, and ultimately for the Crown itself, his feeble reason failed and he became, first temporarily, and then permanently, insane.

Yet before his warlike queen, Margaret of Anjou, and her Lancastrian adherents were finally defeated by the better led and more substantially supported Yorkists, and Henry himself was supplanted on the throne in 1461 by his young warrior cousin, Edward of York, the hapless king bestowed on his country two educational foundations – King's College, Cambridge, and its sister college, the King's College of Our Lady of Eton – where his gentle name is still held in gratitude:

> Here in his realm a realm to found
> Where he might stand for ever crown'd.

The House of York

EDWARD IV

1461—1483

Edward IV was the son of Edward Duke of York, whose own father, a grandson of Edward III, had been beheaded for treason against Henry V. Edward of York was not only the richest magnate in England and, until the unexpected birth of a son to Henry VI in 1453, Heir Presumptive. He was also, as the eldest descendant through the distaff of Lionel of Clarence, the 'legitimate' heir of the pre-Lancastrian Plantagenets. After making himself, by a display of force, Regent of poor, pious Henry VI's chaotic England, and, later, claiming the throne by 'right of descent' – this proud, demanding prince, in the winter of 1460–1, suffered defeat and death at Wakefield at the hands of the Lancastrians. But his nineteen-year-old son, Edward, with the powerful help of his cousin, Richard Neville Earl of Warwick, secured possession of London and had himself proclaimed king. Subsequently he avenged at Towton the Lancastrian victories of Wakefield and St Albans, and forced Henry and his queen to seek refuge in Scotland.

For nearly a decade, with growing success, Edward governed England, which, though passively loyal to the Lancastrian line, welcomed his strong rule and restoration of public order. In 1465 his rival, the crazed, saintly Henry, was captured in the northern wilds and exhibited as a public spectacle before being incarcerated in the Tower. The young Yorkist king who had supplanted him was a magnificent-looking man, nearly six feet four tall, strong, vigorous, handsome and amorous, with a princely charm which won the hearts of men and women. His success with the latter all but proved his undoing, for at the age of twenty-two he bitterly offended his powerful supporter, the Earl of Warwick – then engaged in negotiating a marriage for him with the French king's sister-in-law – by secretly marrying the widow of a Lancastrian knight, Elizabeth, Lady Grey. The subsequent elevation of this beautiful woman's Woodville relations so enraged Warwick that in 1469 he entered into an unnatural alliance with the king's treacherous brother, the Duke of Clarence, and the exiled Lancastrians under Queen Margaret. For a short time 'the King Maker' – as this intensely ambitious man was called – drove Edward from the throne and set up in his place the imbecile, Henry, resurrected from his Tower cell. But Edward, a brilliant soldier, returned to England early in 1471 with the help of his brother-in-law, the Duke of Burgundy, and routed, first Warwick at Barnet, and then Queen Margaret and her young son – whom he put to death after his victory – at Tewkesbury.

For the next twelve years Edward reigned without opposition. A first-class administrator and man of business, he was particularly popular with the trading classes of London to whom the murderous dynastic struggles of the nobility and rival royal houses meant little compared with the maintenance of peace and law. Even the nation's desire for revenge against France he turned to his own and his kingdom's financial advantage, raising in 1474–5 a powerful invading army in conjunction with his ally, the Duke of Burgundy, and then, instead of embarking on another long, ruinous war like his Lancastrian predecessors, accepting from the French king, in return for his peaceful departure, a payment of 75,000 gold crowns and a pension for life.

Edward, who kept great royal state, was a cultured patron of the arts, like his magnificent brother-in-law, the Duke of Burgundy. It was while residing in the latter's dominions, that a London mercer named William Caxton became interested in the new German technique of reproducing books by printing and, on his retirement from Bruges in 1476, set up, in the precincts of Westminster Abbey, the first English printing-press.

EDWARD V

1483

When Edward IV died of a fever at the age of forty, prematurely worn out, it was believed, by his amorous excesses, the Crown descended to his twelve-year-old son, Edward V. This sensitive, intelligent boy who had been living at Ludlow under the care of his Woodville uncle, Earl Rivers, while on his way to London to join his mother, was intercepted by the two greatest magnates of the realm, his father's brother, Richard Duke of Gloucester – 'the King's Lieutenant in the North' – and the Duke of Buckingham. Both, being of royal blood, detested the Queen Mother and her upstart Woodville relations and were determined to wrest the young king from their charge. Gloucester, Edward IV's last surviving brother – for Clarence, attainted for treason, had perished in the Tower – had none of the dead king's flamboyant bonhomie, and was small, introvert, secretive and austere. But he had the same administrative and military skill and courage, and was universally regarded as loyal and trustworthy. He had made himself popular in the wild and formerly Lancastrian North, whose warlike folk he had won over by his firm, but just, rule. Like them, he was reputed to be ruthless and was even said to have murdered Henry VI with his own hands, when in the Tower with him, on the night of the saintly king's death.

This reputation Gloucester now enhanced by summarily arresting, and sending to his northern fastness of Pontefract for later execution, the young king's uncle, Rivers, his half-brother, Lord Richard Grey, and his Chamberlain, Sir Thomas Vaughan. Then, with his royal nephew a virtual prisoner, he marched on London, which he and Buckingham entered on 4 May 1483, four weeks after Edward IV's death, causing the Queen Mother with her daughters and younger son, the nine-year-old Duke of York, to seek sanctuary in the Abbey. Then, at a meeting of the Council, he had himself confirmed as Protector, Defender of the Realm and Guardian of the King's person.

So far his proceedings had met with popular approval. For the Woodvilles were much disliked, and Gloucester seemed better

71

qualified by his rank and experience to rule during the king's minority than anyone else. But it soon appeared that it was not only the Woodvilles of whom he wished to be rid. On 13 June, nine days before the day fixed for the young King's coronation, he suddenly arrested at a Council meeting in the Tower and beheaded without trial his former friend and his dead brother's most trusted adviser, Lord Hastings. Then, having employed a pliant Archbishop of Canterbury to persuade the Queen Mother to allow the little Duke of York to leave sanctuary and join his brother in the Tower, he proceeded to bastardize both brothers by circulating stories that the late king had bigamously married the queen and was even himself illegitimate, thereby casting a slur on his own mother, who was still living.

Having thus, with the help of his ally Buckingham and a number of suborned London preachers, represented himself as the sole remaining legitimate representative of the House of York, on June 26 Richard rode to Westminster Hall and took possession of the throne in the Court of King's Bench. Then, backed by a large armed force from the North, he was crowned King on 6 July. So what little there was of Edward's brief reign was spent in the grim old Tower which William the Conqueror had first raised four centuries before. Nor were he and his brother ever to leave it. For a short while they could be glimpsed by passers-by, playing in the garden; then they disappeared into its inner recesses and were never seen again.

RICHARD III

1483—1485

Soon after his coronation King Richard went on progress to settle his kingdom. From Warwick that August, according to Sir Thomas More – who in his youth had known some of the chief actors in Richard's reign – he despatched one of his henchmen, Sir James Tyrell, to the Governor of the Tower with orders to deliver its keys to him for twenty-four hours. During that time, it was said, two ruffians smothered the royal children and buried them 'at the stair foot . . . under a heap of stones'. The account is open to some doubt, but in 1674, during alterations at the Tower, the skeletons of two boys were found lying on top of one another in this very place. What is certain is that, in the autumn of 1483, ugly rumours began to circulate in both England and France that the princes had been done to death.

If their murder was at Richard's orders, as was widely believed at the time, this otherwise able and astute king committed, not only a shocking crime, but a major political blunder. For though, after thirty years of spasmodic civil war, Englishmen had grown accustomed to their rulers slaughtering one another, the murder of innocent children was something which they could not stomach. For the rest of Richard's brief reign his very real ability was bedevilled by the horror and distrust which the princes' disappearance had aroused, and which he could easily have dispelled had he only been able to produce them – the one thing he had apparently precluded himself from doing. So disastrous was the effect of his inability to do so that he had to face the enmity, not only of the Lancastrians, but of his fellow Yorkists. Before the autumn was out, Richard faced a rising in all the southern counties from Kent to Cornwall. The Woodvilles and Courtenays, the Yorkist bishop of Salisbury, and the Lancastrian Bishops of Exeter and Ely all took part in it. At the end of September they were joined by Richard's former fellow-conspirator, the Duke of Buckingham, who declared himself, not for the displaced boy king he had helped to dethrone but who was now presumed dead, but for the heir of the Lancastrian Beauforts, Henry Tudor Earl of Richmond – an almost unknown twenty-six-year-old Welsh-man living in Brittany, to whom an invitation to assume the throne was now sent in the name of both Yorkists and Lancastrians.

Yet Richard, who never lacked courage, was a formidable warrior. That October, while unprecedented floods prevented the rebels joining forces, with his accustomed speed and daring the king struck down each of his adversaries in turn. Buckingham was executed in Salisbury market-place, and for twenty more uneasy months Richard enjoyed a reprieve. Yet, though he showed himself a generous, munificent and most capable ruler, nothing went right for him. In the spring of 1484 his only son died; in that of 1485 his queen. That summer some doggerel lines on his hated lieutenants, Catesby, Ratcliffe and Lovell and his own heraldic cognizance of the Wild Boar, circulated through the country like wildfire.

> The Cat, the Rat and Lovell our Dog
> Ruleth all England under a Hog

And early in August the long awaited Henry landed in Wales. Before the month was up, though the royal army outnumbered the invader's by two to one, Richard, fighting desperately, met his death on Bosworth Field while half his troops stood idly by or changed sides during the battle because they refused to fight for a man they believed had murdered a helpless child, his own liege lord and brother's heir, whom he had sworn to protect. That night the dead king's crown was picked up from the thorn-bush where it had fallen and set upon Henry Tudor's head.

The House of Tudor

HENRY VII

1485—1509

No king of England ever had a weaker hereditary claim than Henry Tudor; none exercised its powers with more wisdom and success. A Welshman, with his countrymen's flair for combining mysticism with a shrewd eye for the main chance, his father, the Earl of Richmond, had been the offspring of Henry V's French widow by a secret marriage with her clerk of the Wardrobe – an obscure Welsh gentleman named Owen Tudor, later beheaded – while his mother, Margaret Beaufort, through whom he claimed the throne, was granddaughter to one of John of Gaunt's bastard Beaufort sons by his mistress and third wife, Catherine Swynford – Chaucer's sister-in-law. His title was so poor – for the Beauforts, though subsequently legitimized, had been expressly excluded from the succession – that he was reduced to claiming the Crown by virtue of his victory of Bosworth. Yet he remained on the throne for nearly a quarter of a century and, without an army or police force other than his Yeomen of the Guard, defeated every attempt to dethrone him with very little bloodshed except that of rival claimants. By doing so, and by his marriage with Edward IV's eldest daughter, Elizabeth of York, he ended the Wars of the Roses.

Henry VII was perhaps the cleverest, and certainly the hardest-working, man to wear the English crown. He started his reign heavily in debt and ended it, long after he had repaid all his creditors, richer than any king before. He used his wealth, so industriously accumulated and carefully husbanded – for he audited and signed almost every page of his accounts himself – to increase the royal power and free it from incumbrances and restraints. Habituated from his perilous childhood, and by his penurious years of exile, to keeping his cards close to his chest, he was described by his biographer, Francis Bacon, as 'the secretest man' that lived.

To end the tyranny of 'the overmighty subject', especially the over-mighty subject with the heady and perilous temptation of royal blood in his veins, Henry invested the Crown with a new mystique, setting it as a thing apart, in its lonely majesty, from the subject. With only one duke and one marquis left after the holocausts and attainders of the Wars of the Roses, he chose his councillors mostly from new men who depended solely on himself, and used his Council, the Court of the Star Chamber and the Councils of the Marches and the North, to discipline the ambitious, rich and powerful who employed power and wealth to pervert the course of justice. Under these he governed an England, long used to turbulence, through the unpaid local magistracy which Edward I had first created and on which, by his successive Commissions of the Peace, Henry laid ever-increasing burdens.

Though he taxed his subjects unrelentingly, he enabled them to grow rich like himself. His reign was notable, more even than that of Edward IV, for the rapid increase in wealth of the merchant classes, particularly of those engaged in the great national industry of cloth-making which, during the fifteenth century, was taking the place of the export of wool as the country's chief commercial activity. It saw the rise of splendid Perpendicular churches in all the cloth-working districts, of new forms of domestic architecture more suitable to a peaceful trading than to a warlike feudal society, and the final flowering of England's Gothic ecclesiastical architecture. The noblest examples of it were the royal foundations – for, like all the Lancastrians, Henry was devout and orthodox – of the magnificent chantry chapel in Westminster Abbey which bears his name and in which he was buried, and the wonderful interior of King's College Chapel, Cambridge, which he provided for in his Will as a memorial to his saintly Lancastrian predecessor, Henry VI.

HENRY VIII

1509—1547

Where Henry VII was circumspect, secretive, parsimonious and unceasingly industrious, his son was an extrovert, bursting with self-confidence, extravagant and avid for pleasure. Succeeding to the throne at eighteen, he was a superlatively handsome, accomplished, and, at first, immensely popular Renaissance prince.

Longing to shine he at once started to get through his father's accumulated treasure by engaging in costly foreign adventures, including war with France. But unlike an earlier 'King Hal', he sought the palm and not the dust, and the highlight of his campaigning was the Field of the Cloth of Gold in which he vied with the French king in extravagant magnificence. Intent on his pleasures, for the first twenty years of his reign he left the management of his kingdom's affairs to a brilliant churchman of humble birth, Thomas Wolsey, who rose to be the richest and most powerful man in the country, Lord Chancellor, Archbishop of York, a Cardinal and, later, Papal Legate.

Yet there was one problem to which, even in those years of pleasure and display, the king was forced to give his mind – that of the succession. For his Spanish wife, Catherine of Aragon – to whom his father had affianced him after the death of his elder brother, her boy husband – gave him only one surviving child, a daughter born in 1515. When it became clear that she could never bear another, Henry, who had to provide for the country's future security, sought a papal annulment of his marriage. Accustomed to having his way in all things, he was also deeply in love – 'stricken', as he put it, 'with the dart of love' – with a *femme fatale*, Anne Boleyn, granddaughter of a rich London merchant, whose price was marriage.

For several years Henry and his minister, Wolsey, importuned the Vatican for a divorce. An orthodox champion of the Roman Church against the new Protestant heresies now raging on the Continent, he would have had little difficulty in obtaining one had not his Queen been aunt to the most powerful Catholic monarch of the time, the Emperor Charles V, on whose goodwill the Pope was dependent against the French invaders of Italy. Thwarted, Henry finally got his way by breaking with the Papacy, dismissing Wolsey, and appointing as Archbishop of Canterbury a married churchman, Thomas Cranmer, who set up a Court which pronounced Catherine divorced, so enabling the king to make Anne his queen.

During the fifteen-thirties Henry and his new minister, Thomas Cromwell – a lawyer of Protestant sympathies completely dependent on the king – carried through, with the help of a strongly anti-clerical Parliament, the most drastic revolution in English history. Declaring, in an Act against Appeals to Rome, that the realm of England was 'an empire . . . governed by one supreme Head and King', they ended all links with the Papacy, constituted the king supreme head of the Church of England, and dissolved the monasteries, confiscating their enormous wealth. Yet, though Henry broke with Rome and ruthlessly suppressed a North Country rising in support of the monasteries, he never accepted the doctrinal and theological tenets of the Protestant reformers. He executed both Anne Boleyn, who failed to give him a son, and Cromwell, as he also did another of his six successive wives, and persecuted as heretics all who deviated from Catholic orthodox belief. During his last years he was sole and absolute master of his kingdom, and, though striking terror into all who dared oppose him, remained, in spite of his personal despotism, immensely popular with his subjects. A patron of seamen like his father, his reign saw the first beginnings of a permanent Royal Navy, of a Navy Board to supply and control it, and of warships built, instead of hired, for permanent employment by the Crown.

EDWARD VI

1547—1553

When Henry VIII died in 1547 the chickens hatched under his despotic and wilful rule came home to roost on the throne of his nine-year-old son, Edward. These were an empty Treasury, inflation engendered by reckless expenditure on foreign wars and an unscrupulous debasement of the currency, and popular unrest and bitterness caused by a generation of heartless enclosure and get-rich-quick land-grabbers and money-makers acting without regard to social justice. Above all, there were the growing religious differences unloosed by an as yet purely royal and parliamentary Reformation which had destroyed the links and disciplines of long Catholic habitude while retaining an enforced conformity to outworn, and increasingly questioned, religious assumptions and beliefs.

The only outstanding question as yet settled was the succession, and that only precariously. For, though by one of his wives, Jane Seymour, who died in childbirth in 1537, Henry had at last achieved a son, he bequeathed him but a feeble constitution. Of his two daughters, the elder, Mary, was a devoted Catholic, eager to undo what her father had done, while the younger, Elizabeth – child of Anne Boleyn – inclined to the reformed beliefs. And though their succession, in the event of Edward predeceasing them without heirs, had been provided for by Henry's Act of Settlement, both were women, and therefore considered by most people incapable of ruling a turbulent and divided realm.

Though the old king, seeking to rule from the grave, had hoped to preserve the religious *status quo* he had established, the councillors he appointed to act during his son's minority allowed the reforming elements in the Church and laity a freedom hitherto denied. Chief among them was the boy king's uncle, Edward Seymour Duke of Somerset – a hero of the Scottish and French wars – who constituted himself Protector. Under his tolerant aegis English Protestants in exile were allowed to return from the Continent and the clergy to marry, while Communion in both kinds took the place of Mass, and the anti-heresy laws were repeated by Parliament. Henry had already licensed the publication of an English Bible in the hope of checking the clandestine circulation of unauthorized translations. The Archbishop of Canterbury, Thomas Cranmer, now issued in 1549 his Book of Common Prayer, which endowed the Church of England and the English people with the lovely cadences and consoling wisdom of its incomparable liturgy.

Though like everyone else in power, Somerset feathered his own nest, he was genuinely anxious to redress the social wrongs from which the poor were suffering through enclosure, inflation and the dissolution of the monasteries. Unfortunately, by attempting to do so too quickly he aroused such unruly hopes in the rough uneducated common people that they rose in rebellion, so provoking a violent reaction which led to his supersession – and ultimate execution – by a far more ruthless and ambitious dictator, John Dudley Duke of Northumberland. But, though during the last three years of the reign the latter enjoyed complete control of the Council and young king – a brilliantly precocious but, as his diary showed, cold and reserved prig – his plans for excluding the Catholic Princess Mary from the succession in favour of Lady Jane Grey, a sixteen-year-old Protestant great-granddaughter of Henry VII affianced to his son, were thwarted by Edward's death of consumption at the age of fifteen.

MARY I

1553—1558

Mary Tudor's reign was almost the saddest in English history, both for herself and her people. The daughter of Henry VIII and his divorced Spanish wife, she had suffered deeply from her father's treatment of her mother and his schismatical breach with the Church of her forebears. Child of a princess of Spain she was a cousin to the greatest monarch since the days of imperial Rome – the Emperor Charles V, who was lord of Spain, the Netherlands, half Germany and Italy and of the immense wealth of the New World. When after years of insults and humiliations her half-brother's failing health made her accession to the throne imminent she, who had once been bastardized by her own father, became at thirty-seven a match even for Charles V's heir, Philip of Spain, who was seeking to weave England into the web of Spanish dynastic marriages and so align her in his war against France. For Mary, who had suffered so many years of loneliness and whose dearest wish was to restore her erring country after twenty years of schism to its former Faith, marriage with the crusading champion of the Counter-Reformation and earth's greatest monarch seemed a dazzling prospect.

Mary was kindly, charitable, affectionate, scrupulously honest – an un-Tudor trait – and excessively devout. She was also, like all her family, brave and stubborn, most of all in defence of her religion. When in the days of the Protestant triumph after her brother's accession, the Bishop of London – whom afterwards she burnt at the stake – had called on her to adopt the new Prayer Book and expressed the hope that she would not 'refuse God's word', she replied, 'I cannot tell what ye call God's word; that is not God's word now that was God's word in my father's days ... You durst not for your ears have avouched that for God's word in my father's days'.

At the time of her accession, Mary enjoyed the loyalty of her people, even those who had accepted the new religion – still then only a minority. When the brutal and ambitious Duke of Northumberland raised a rebellion and proclaimed Lady Jane Grey in her place, the country rallied instantaneously to the Queen.

But the enthusiasm soon evaporated. The marriage to Philip of Spain, who made a brief visit to England to wed her but never returned again, proved intensely unpopular with an insular people, and for Mary a barren and cruel disappointment. At thirty-seven, with failing health, she was prematurely old, and the cold, correct Philip and his arrogant Spanish courtiers made no bones about it; 'What', one of them asked, 'shall the king do with such an old bitch?' Her hopes of a child, desperately sustained until time and her husband's continued absence made it impossible, proved a chimera.

All the Queen had left was her religion and her fierce Tudor resolve to re-impose it on her heretic subjects. Innocent of the world out of which she had so long lived, and ill-advised – particularly by her cousin, Cardinal Pole, who returned from exile to aid her in her self-imposed task – she went about it in the worst possible way. As well as having the leading Protestant churchmen, Archbishop Cranmer and Bishops Ridley and Latimer, burnt at the stake, she authorized, during her last three years, the burning of some three hundred humble Protestants, more than fifty of them women. This atrocious business, carried out in public, had an effect on the English very different to that which their queen intended. For if the loss of Calais – the last relic of England's Plantagenet conquests – whose capture by France in 1558 was the only tangible result of the Spanish marriage and alliance – the memory of the Smithfield martyrs, more than any single factor, made the English people for three centuries the undeviating enemies of Rome.

ELIZABETH I

1558—1603

No sovereign ever served a harder apprenticeship than Elizabeth. Hardly before she was out of her cradle her terrifying father had executed her mother, Anne Boleyn, and declared her illegitimate. Her first admirer, a married man of forty and brother to the Lord Protector Somerset, was executed for courting her – a lesson which taught her how dangerous it was for a woman in her position to indulge her affections. In an age of treachery and violence, when an occupant of, or aspirant to, the throne had every incentive to eliminate rivals, her life was in constant danger. Soon after the accession of her half-sister Mary, she was thrown into the Tower and subjected to almost daily cross-examination. Only her cool head and stout heart saved her.

Superbly educated – she was widely-read and mistress of six languages, including Latin and Greek – her accession at the age of twenty-five came as a providential deliverance to her Protestant subjects and herself. She played it as the first act of a drama which was to continue to her dying day. A magnificent actress who well knew how to hide her thoughts and feelings, there was no doubt of the sincerity with which she identified herself with her people. 'Have a care over them', she wrote to her judges, 'do you that which I ought to do. They are my people. Every man oppresseth and spoileth them without mercy. See unto them, see unto them, as they are my charge'. 'Far above all earthly treasures', she declared many years later, 'I esteem my people's love'. 'You may well have a greater prince', she told them, 'you shall never have a more loving one'.

The reign, a forty-five years' love affair between Elizabeth and her people, began with great hazards for both. 'The Queen poor', a contemporary wrote, 'the realm exhausted; the nobles poor and decayed; good captains and soldiers wanting; the people out of order; justice not executed; . . . all things dear; division among ourselves; war with France and Scotland; the French king bestriding the realm; steadfast enmity but no steadfast friendship abroad'. England, a weak half-island on the fringe of a continent dominated by two great Catholic powers, was shut out from the trade and wealth of the New World by the Pope's decrees and the naval might of Spain and Portugal.

Elizabeth and her ministers, whom she chose with great shrewdness, played for time: time for her people to resolve their religious discords, to reform the currency, to solve the problems of poverty and unemployment, to recover national unity, above all to grow strong enough to meet the challenge of the immense foreign forces threatening them. She played it with cunning, equivocation, parsimony, constant delays and every womanly and queenly art with which she was endowed, and, when the crunch could no longer be avoided, with magnificent courage. 'I thank God', she told her Parliament, 'that I am imbued with such qualities that if I were turned out of the realm in my petticoat, I were able to live in any place in Christendom'.

Her people caught her courage, none more so than the West Country seamen whose voyages of discovery, trade and piracy into forbidden oceans paved the way for the foundation of the British Empire. Drake's voyage round the world in 1577–80 – culminating in the queen, a shareholder, knighting him on the deck of the *Golden Hind* – is one of the great epics of history. Eight years later, when the 'Invincible Armada' struck, it was Elizabeth who told her troops that, though she had the body of a weak, feeble woman, she had the heart and stomach of a king, and of a King of England too, and thought foul scorn that . . . any Prince of Europe should dare to invade the borders of her realm. And it was Drake and his fellow sea-dogs who ensured that none should do so, predicting, as he drummed the Spaniards up the Channel, 'I doubt not so to handle the matter with the Duke of Sidonia as he shall wish himself at St Mary Port among his orange trees'.

The House of Stuart

JAMES I

1603—1625

James VI of Scotland who, on Elizabeth's death and with her belated assent, became James I of England, was the only son of Mary Queen of Scots – a great-granddaughter of Henry VII – who, first married to Francis II of France, bore James in 1566 by her second, and subsequently murdered, husband, Henry Stuart, Lord Darnley. An ardent Catholic, unlike her Scottish subjects who had embraced the Calvinist form of Protestantism with stern enthusiasm, and driven by them from her realm shortly after her son's birth, she had fled for refuge to England, where for twenty years, imprisoned in Fotheringhay Castle, she had been the focus of every Catholic and foreign plot to assassinate Elizabeth, until in 1587, on the eve of the Armada, the latter authorized her execution.

Brought up, an orphan in his mother's absence, as a Protestant, James, unlike her, constituted no threat to the reformed religion in England. Yet he was no Presbyterian like his Scottish subjects, against whose democratic Church government and discipline he reacted vehemently, as he did against those who wished to abolish episcopacy in his new kingdom. 'No bishop, no king!', was a favourite saying of his. Though at first received with enthusiasm by the English, his strongly expressed dislike of parliamentary criticism soon caused a rift between them.

A scholar, who published two books on the theory of authoritarian kingship, and an incorrigible pedant whose dearest wish was to be 'the great schoolmaster of the whole land', James strongly resented the reluctance of his new people's elected representatives to vote him supplies without redress of grievances. He assured Parliament, after the discovery of the Catholic Gunpowder Plot of 1605, that kings were 'God's vice-regents on earth and so adorned and furnished with some sparkles of the Divinity'. 'The House of Commons is a body without a head' he told the Spanish ambassador with whose king, much to the disgust of his subjects, he was trying to negotiate an alliance. 'At their meetings nothing is heard but cries, shouts and confusion. I am surprised that my ancestors should ever have permitted such an institution to have come into existence'. 'He that will have all done by Parliament', he declared on another occasion, 'is an enemy to monarchy and a traitor to the King of England'.

This attitude, and the pedantry with which he proclaimed it, increasingly alienated his English subjects, as did his bumbling lack of dignity and doting dependence on unworthy favourites like the unsavoury Robert Carr, who was involved with his wife in a murder scandal, and the overweeningly ambitious George Villiers whom he made Duke of Buckingham and Lord High Admiral. Yet James was too shrewd to press matters to extremes with his Parliaments, and the constitutional and religious problems raised by his reign did not explode in his time Its chief products – apart from Shakespeare's tragedies and last comedies – were the publication in 1611, following the Hampton Court Conference of divines, of the magnificent Authorized Version of the Bible, which was to become the chief educational influence in the nation's life for the next three centuries; and the earliest English settlements in North America. The first of these, Virginia, was founded by a London trading company in 1606, and the second, Massachusetts, in 1620 by a small group of Puritan enthusiasts, who, sailing from Plymouth in the 180-ton *Mayflower*, resolved to live or die in the perilous transatlantic wilderness rather than conform to a, to them, tyrannical episcopal and doctrinal discipline at home.

CHARLES I

1625—1649

Charles I was born in Scotland, and only came to England when he was four. His mother was a Dane, and, though himself a staunch episcopalian Protestant, he married a French Catholic princess. Understanding of the people he was called upon to govern came to him only very gradually. He was a delicate child with weak legs and an impediment in speech, which only a strong will enabled him to overcome. But he remained always sparing of words – and, 'when he was warm in discourse, inclined to stammer' – and, being secretive and reserved in manner, the warmth of his affections was only shown to his close intimates, in particular his wife and children and the friend of his youth, 'Steenee' Villiers, Duke of Buckingham.

Charles became heir to the throne on his brother, Henry's, death in 1612. At twenty-four he succeeded his father, whose academic belief in the Divine Right of kings he shared with almost mystical conviction. During the first four years of his reign he became embroiled with three successive Parliaments, whose claims to control policy and criticize his ministers he regarded as treasonable, and whose reluctance to grant taxes he bitterly resented. After 1629 he governed the country for eleven years by proclamation without calling a Parliament. His intentions were benevolent – for he was essentially a good man – but, unlike the far more autocratic Tudors, he completely failed to appreciate Edward I's dictum that that which touches all should be approved by all, and that to govern England effectively there must be 'counsel and consent'. By identifying the Crown with the exercise of untrammelled administrative authority – in that age frequently corrupt, occasionally unjust and nearly always inefficient – and with ideological and religious notions antipathetic to a majority of his people, he undermined the instinctive love of the nation for its hereditary monarchy.

A man of rare artistic feeling and perception – he was a great collector of paintings and sculpture – Charles was a thoroughly bad politician. A poor judge of character, he lacked flexibility and shrewdness and had little sense of timing. His favourite churchman, Archbishop Laud, described him as 'a mild and gracious prince who knew not how to be or be made great'. Having blundered into an unnecessary war with his Presbyterian Scottish subjects by trying to impose bishops on them, in 1640 he was forced by lack of money to call a Parliament. The cumulative undercurrent of criticism which he had so long dammed became a raging torrent, and, backed by the London mob, his parliamentary opponents were able to compel him, among other distasteful things, to give up his right of dissolution and to sign the death warrant of his faithful Minister, Strafford. Finally, rather than surrender his control of the Militia, he appealed to arms, the conservative North and West of the country loyally supporting him, while the richer and more populous South-East and the capital backed Parliament.

In four years' civil war, helped by the Scots and a professional 'New Model' army, Parliament was victorious. But though Charles was forced to concede every parliamentary demand, so fanatical was his belief in his hereditary right to govern that he would not be bound by any concession. And though Parliament, Scotland and the Army fell out and, as a result of the king's intrigues, became embroiled in a second Civil War, the ultimate victors – the Army chiefs – reluctantly resolved on his death as the only way of preserving the war's gains. Yet by putting Charles on trial in Westminster Hall, they enabled him to challenge, publicly and with great eloquence, their legal right to try him. By this, and his superb dignity on the scaffold, he saved – at the loss of his head – both the Crown and the Church of England, which, by his earlier obduracy, he had brought to the point of ruin. 'I do stand more for the liberty of my people', he declared, 'than any here that come to be my pretended judges, and therefore let me know by what lawful authority I am seated here . . . For if power without law may make law, may alter the fundamental laws of the kingdom, I know not what subject he is in England can be assured of his life or anything he can call his own'.

CROMWELL

1649—1658

(INTERREGNUM 1649-1660)

Oliver Cromwell, a Huntingdonshire squire of Fenland and Welsh ancestry, was born in 1599. He was educated at the great Puritan Cambridge college, Sidney Sussex, and represented Huntingdon in Parliament. A fellow member recalled him speaking there in 1640 in a plain cloth suit made by an ill country tailor; 'his sword stuck close to his side, his countenance swollen and reddish, his voice sharp and untunable and his eloquence full of fervour'.

When the civil war broke out he raised a troop of horse for the Parliament from his country neighbours whose cause he had championed against rich royal concessioners. An impassioned Puritan, he recruited men of like religious convictions, regardless of rank or wealth, 'such as had the fear of God before them and made some conscience of what they did!' 'I had rather', he said, 'have a plain russet-coated captain that knows what he fights for and loves what he knows, than that which you call a gentleman and is nothing else'.

He proved a cavalry commander of genius and led the decisive charges at Marston Moor and Naseby, later playing a major part in the Army's negotiations with Charles I. It was his realization of the latter's intransigence which made him decide Charles must die. 'We will cut off his head with the crown upon it', he told his fellow officers.

After the King's death Cromwell found himself, as the chief link between Parliament and the Army, and the one man whom the latter trusted, increasingly called upon to direct the destinies of the new republic or Commonwealth. In 1649, as Commander-in-Chief in Ireland, he ended a cruel and interminable racial and religious war by storming Drogheda and Wexford and putting their stubborn garrisons to the sword. In 1650, when the Scots invited the young king in exile, Charles II, to Scotland, Cromwell routed them at Dunbar, and a year later, after they had invaded western England, at Worcester. In 1653 he intervened decisively

93

in politics by turning out the corrupt remnant or 'Rump' of the oft-purged Long Parliament, and assumed the title of Protector, seeing himself, as he said, as 'set upon a watch-tower to see what may be for the good of this nation, and what may be for the prevention of evil'.

For five years Cromwell was virtually dictator. Being an Englishman with a respect for legality, he was not happy. Nor, though he wished to see England the kind of land he and his Puritan soldiers had dreamed of, and fought for, did he believe this could be achieved by letting unrealistic fanatics – Agitators, Levellers, Anabaptists – set up an egalitarian Utopia without rule, order, or social stability. Despite the intensity of his Puritan idealism, Cromwell was a realist. The paradox of his position – and of the nation whose underlying instincts he represented – was that, having fought to destroy the unparliamentary rule of Charles I, he came eventually to realize that the only kind of state in which Englishmen could be happy was that of a constitutional monarchy in which personal liberty and property were assured under the rule of law. 'A nobleman, a gentleman, a yeoman', he said, 'that is a good interest of a nation, and a great one'.

For Cromwell, the Puritan revolutionary who set out to

'cast the kingdoms old
into another mould',

was at heart a conservative who wished to conserve and ultimately – though he did not realize it – restore the English polity which the Stuart kings and the nation's reaction against them had destroyed. All his attempts to end his own military dictatorship by setting up checks and balances – the 'Praise-God Barebones' Parliament of 'the Saints', the Instrument of Government, the rule of the Major-Generals – ended in failure. When in 1658 he died, after reluctantly refusing the proffered Crown, it became clear, during an eighteen months' anarchic interregnum of warring major generals, that nothing could meet England's need but the restoration of Crown and Parliament.

CHARLES II

1660—1685

Charles II had begun his nominal reign at eighteen as the exiled head of a faction of broken men, debts and beggary. Then the tempter had appeared in the guise of a Presbyterian elder and offered him the Scottish crown in return for the renunciation of the episcopal cause for which his father had died. There followed a year of long Scots' sermons, mortifications and salutary corrections. Yet an interlude, begun in shame, ended, though with defeat and peril of death, in romance. After a wild dash into England his outnumbered army was routed at Worcester. For six weeks a fugitive, with a price on his head, Charles was as much part of England as the October hedges. A family of poor Catholic wood-cutters sheltered him. A hunted priest smuggled him into the proud and willing custody of a ruined royalist house, whose daughter, Jane Lane, carried for a week the Crown of England in her hands – and never was trust more faithfully performed. After many perils and hardships, a ship was found for France.

Once more Charles became the shadow of a king – so thin and attenuated that his enemies in England could forget him. His was a world of poor, ruined Cavaliers, wandering from one debt-haunted corner of Europe to another and begging their bread from contemptuous princes. In 1660, when night seemed darkest, General Monck marched, and in London 'a fellow came with a ladder upon his shoulder and a pot of paint in his hand and set the ladder in the place where the late king's statue had stood and . . . wiped out that inscription, *"Exit Tyrannus"* and, as soon as he had done it, threw up his cap and cried, *"God bless King Charles the Second"* – in which the whole Exchange joined with the joyfullest shout you can imagine'. When a free Parliament met and the king's message from Breda was read, a nation, weary of the rule of saints, bigots and major-generals, went mad with joy. And on May 29, with all London greeting the returning 'Black Boy', the diarist Evelyn 'stood in the Strand and beheld it and blessed God. It was the Lord's doing, for such a restoration was never mentioned in any history'. And from that hour, as the rector

95

of Maid's Moreton recorded, 'ancient orders began to be observed'.

Taught in a hard school of poverty and vagabondage, Charles was without illusions. Possessing energy, a superb constitution and a keen appreciation of pleasure, he was ready to enjoy both the duties and amusements of his changed situation. He had had a bad time and meant to have a good one. Above all, he was determined 'not to go on his travels again'. 'A pleasure called sauntering was the true sultana queen he delighted in'. He liked to come and go at his ease and have his movements unconfined. 'He loved a smart walk, a mouthful of fresh air and a little ingenious raillery . . . He walked by his watch and, when he pulled it out, skilful men would make haste with what they had to say to him'.

Yet, unlike his father, when driven to it, Charles was a superb politician. When the whole nation lost its head over the pretended Popish Plot, he kept his and preserved the hereditary succession. His Parliaments were often factious and invariably kept him short of money, yet in the end, with the help of a secret subsidy from his cousin, Louis XIV – for which, cynically and characteristically, he gave nothing tangible in return – he was able to govern the country without parliamentary aid on a broad basis of popular loyalty.

Charles's reign was attended by two major disasters – the Plague of 1665 and the Fire of London, which in 1666 destroyed two-thirds of the capital. Yet during the next nineteen years the country grew richer, and its maritime commerce expanded more quickly, than ever before. 'The thing which is nearest the heart of this nation', Charles told his sister, 'is trade and all that belongs to it', and his realization of it enabled his people to help themselves.

JAMES II

1685—1688

Unlike his brother, Charles, who was dark, James was fair with a long lantern-jaw and a stolid, mulish and phlegmatic temperament. Born in 1633, he had heard, while still a boy, the London mob howling for Strafford's blood, seen the defeat of his father's armies and been imprisoned by the victorious Parliament in the old palace of St James's, whence he had escaped to the Continent in a Thames barge disguised as a girl. For twelve years he was an exile, earning his living as a soldier in the wars of France and Spain, both of whose armies in the Netherlands he at one time temporarily commanded as deputy for their commanders.

In May 1660 the Duke of York, as he then was, returned to England as Heir Presumptive and Lord High Admiral – an office in which for the next twelve years he directed the country's naval affairs, commanding her fleet in two great naval engagements against the Dutch. But in 1672, having publicly embraced the hated Roman Catholic faith, he was forced to relinquish office, and, a few years later, during the so-called Popish Plot, to face a widespread popular demand for his exclusion from the succession in favour of Charles II's Protestant bastard, the Duke of Monmouth. Living for a time, on account of his intense unpopularity, in exile, he was recalled by his brother to his old charge in 1684 when, and after his accession in the following year, through the agency of the great naval administrator, Samuel Pepys, he did more to strengthen the Royal Navy than any other English sovereign.

Yet in his three and a half years' reign, by his tactlessness, inability to compromise, and the rigidity with which he sought to extend the rights of his fellow co-religionists and break the Anglican Church's state monopoly, he threw away all the advantages won by his brother's political skill. Acclaimed by the ruling High Tory party as the son of the martyred king who had died for the Church of England, he persisted in outraging its most cherished beliefs and prejudices by unilaterally suspending the laws in order to grant office to Roman Catholics and Dissenters, by governing without a Parliament – since no Parliament would endorse his policy – and by maintaining a standing army partly recruited from Irish Papists and destined, it was popularly believed, to enslave the nation. When in the summer of 1688 a son was unexpectedly born to his second and Catholic queen, Mary of Modena, abandoning the hope that their dilemma was only temporary and putting their religion before their loyalty, James's disillusioned Tory supporters joined with their Whig opponents in secretly inviting his Protestant son-in-law, William of Orange, to invade England to save the religion and laws of the country. This William did, landing at Torbay in November, with the aid of 'a Protestant wind' and a Dutch fleet and army.

Betrayed by those whom he most trusted, including his daughters, Mary of Orange and Anne, James lost his head and, for once, his courage, and after five weeks of uncertainty, retreat and confusion, unsuccessfully attempted to flee the country. He thereby gave those who wished, not merely to restrain, but to dethrone him, the chance to declare the Crown vacant. A second attempt to escape – encouraged by William – proved successful, and at three o'clock on the morning of Christmas Day, 1688, the hapless king landed in France, never to return to England. He thus helped to ensure that the 'great and glorious Revolution', which finally established the supremacy of Parliament, was also bloodless.

WILLIAM and MARY
1689—1702   1689—1694

There had been three parties to the Revolution of 1688: James, who had precipitated it by suspending the laws against Catholics and Dissenters; the English people, who forty years earlier had beheaded his father for attempting to govern without Parliament; and Prince William of Orange – Captain-General or Stadtholder of the Dutch Republic – James's nephew and son-in-law. Yet William had not risked his life and a Dutch fleet and army merely to limit the prerogative powers of the English Crown, to which his own wife, James's daughter, had been until that summer heir presumptive. He had come to ensure that the maritime kingdom, which sixteen years before, with Louis XIV's France, had attacked his native Netherlands, should join in the great European alliance which it was his life's work to build against French aggression. Convinced that he was designed by Providence to contain and defeat the Grand Monarque's drive to universal hegemony, this spare, sallow, reserved man of thirty-eight, with his eagle's nose and eye and the blood of his great-grandfather, William the Silent, had by his daring invasion of England driven from her throne the Catholic king who might have taken her into the French camp. He therefore made it plain to his English hosts that, if they wished him to continue to preserve them from civil war, anarchy or a return of James from exile with the French at his back, it would have to be as king, and not merely as regent for his absent father-in-law or prince consort to his wife. And that if he accepted the crown, his new kingdom would have to support his grand design for reducing the swollen power of France.

The upshot was a compact between the two successful partners in 'the Glorious Revolution'. When in January 1689 the 'free Parliament' or Convention, which William had come to ensure for the English people, met, the latter's representatives offered him and his wife – both grandchildren of Charles I – the crown during their joint lives and the life of the survivor, with the 'sole and full exercise of the regal power' vested in William, which meant, under existing constitutional practice, control of the country's foreign policy. But the offer was made conditional on the new Sovereign's acceptance of a Declaration of Rights 'to secure the rights, laws and liberties of the nation'. This declared illegal all those claims and acts by which James had tried to exercise autocratic power without consent of Parliament – the prerogative-power of suspending or dispensing with the laws, interference with the freedom of elections and of parliamentary speech and debate, the prosecution of subjects for petitioning, and the raising and maintenance by the Crown acting alone of a standing army. When subsequently the Convention constituted itself a legal Parliament, this Declaration was embodied in a formal Bill of Rights which ensured beyond all further dispute that henceforward no monarch could govern England except through Parliament and under the rule of law.

The conditional grant of the Crown to William and Mary marked the beginning of that long series of naval, military, commercial and colonial wars between England and France which were to occupy more than half the next 126 years. The first of them, which lasted till 1697, saw William's victory of the Boyne and the failure of the French to establish James in Ireland, the defeat of the French fleet at La Hogue, and the death in 1694 of Mary, leaving William to govern England alone until his death in 1702.

ANNE
1702—1714

On William's death the throne passed to his sister-in-law, the Princess Anne – a stout, middle-aged, fretful, affectionate and essentially ordinary woman, fond of her food, whom the chief poet of her reign enshrined in the lines,

> Here thou, great Anna! whom three realms obey,
> Dost sometimes counsel take – and sometimes tea.

Born in the plague year of 1665, she was the younger daughter of James II's first wife and a granddaughter of Charles II's Chancellor, Edward Hyde Earl of Clarendon, whose majestic *History of the Rebellion and Civil Wars* was published at the beginning of her reign. She had married at eighteen Prince George of Denmark, of whom Charles II had said that he had 'tried him drunk and tried him sober, but that, drunk or sober, there was nothing in him'. None of her children survived infancy save one, William Duke of Gloucester, and, as he, too, died at the age of eleven, the question of the succession remained wide open. The obvious 'legitimate' candidate was Anne's young half-brother, the thirteen-year-old James – known to history as the Old Pretender – who, on his father's death in exile in 1701, called himself James III, but who, being a Catholic, was barred from England's Protestant throne by the Bill of Rights and Act of Settlement.

If Anne was mediocre, her closest confidante and adored friend, and chief Lady of the Bedchamber, was anything but. Sarah Countess of Marlborough was the most forceful Englishwoman of her age, and was married to the country's greatest soldier and diplomat, John Churchill Earl of Marlborough, who, on King William's death, had succeeded to his task of keeping the Grand Alliance against Louis XIV in being. For in 1702 war with France broke out again over Louis's acceptance for his grandson of the vacant throne of Spain, with all its immense territorial possessions in Central and Southern America. Raised to a dukedom by the queen and appointed Commander-in-Chief of the British and Allied Forces in the Low Countries 'as the most proper person in all her dominions to conduct her armies, . . . a man of cool head and warm heart, fit to encounter the genius of France and strangle her designs of swallowing Europe', Marlborough in 1704 staggered the world, and placed his country on the highest pinnacle of fame, by his daring march to the Danube and annihilating victory of Blenheim. Admiral Rooke's capture in the same year of Gibraltar, with its key to command of the Mediterranean, and Marlborough's later victories in the Low Countries of Ramillies, Oudenarde and Malplaquet made England, though with only a third of France's population, the decisive power in Europe.

During Anne's reign England first became conscious of her destiny. Before that she had had great moments, but they had been short-lived, like the triumphs of Edward III and Henry V, Elizabeth and Cromwell. But now beyond the island mists, within reach of a little nation which was learning to use its vantage-point at the ocean gates of Europe, lay a prospect of wealth and maritime power such as no people had ever hitherto enjoyed. 'He calls the sea the British common', Queen Anne's subject, Joseph Addison, wrote of his imaginary merchant, Sir Andrew Freeport; 'there is not a point in the compass but blows home a ship in which he is an owner'. The English – and with them the Scots, whose Parliament, following the union of the two Crowns a century earlier, had now been joined with England's by the Act of Union of 1707 – began to seize their opportunities with both hands.

The House of Hanover

GEORGE I

1714—1727

'When George in pudding time came o'er', sang the Vicar of Bray, 'and moderate men looked big, Sir, my politics I changed once more and so became a Whig, Sir'. It was precisely this that Britain did when Queen Anne died in 1714 of dropsy. As the only alternative to a Catholic and Stuart king, an intensely Protestant nation repudiated the Tory leaders – who had been governing England during the Queen's last years, and the more extreme of whom, fearful for their future, had been flirting with the Pretender over the water – and sent for the Elector of Hanover, a great-grandson of James I by his daughter, Elizabeth Queen of Bohemia, and on whose heirs Parliament had settled the throne in the event of Anne dying childless.

It was not an inspiring choice, but no other was available. George I was a short, blonde, choleric German princeling, with rolling, projecting blue eyes and scarcely a word of English. For the past twenty years he had kept his unfaithful wife locked up in a castle in Hanover where she remained until her death, and he was on the worst of terms with his son and heir. He brought with him two regular mistresses, a tall, scraggy, bony one named von Schulenburg whom he made Duchess of Kendal, and the other, Kielmannsegge, who was immensely fat and became Countess of Darlington. Both were rapacious and made the best of their changed circumstances.

Yet, though the English did not take with enthusiasm to their new Sovereign and his family, and though his first year on the throne saw an unsuccessful Scottish rising in favour of the Old Pretender, they accepted the dynasty with stolid resignation. Divided during the previous century by violent political and religious controversies, with the Revolution of 1688 they had achieved a working compromise and, with it, national unity. Its essence was that Englishmen should cease to destroy one another for the sake of abstract theories and seek a working compromise upon which they could agree to differ. Moderation, distrust of fanaticism, toleration – except for Papists – and liberty preserved by rational laws and the sanctity of property, formed the eighteenth-century national recipe for well-being.

It worked. So did the parliamentary government of the country under the new dynastic set-up. Partly because the king found it difficult to understand English and partly because of his quarrels with the Prince of Wales who could, he ceased to preside over the Cabinet meetings of his Ministers as Queen Anne and William III had done. Instead, he left that duty to his first or – as he came to be called – Prime Minister. After a series of unsuccessful experiments with one intriguing Whig magnate after another, George, who was not without shrewdness, lighted on the ideal man to perform this function – a large, bluff, dominating, bucolic Norfolk squire, Sir Robert Walpole, who rose to power by the adroitness with which he defended the Court – and in particular the King's mistresses and his own fellow Ministers – from public outcry after the collapse in 1720 of the South Sea Bubble, a national financial scandal in which almost everyone in high place was involved. With his bonhomie and cynical understanding of human nature, he had a genius for managing the House of Commons. He used the Crown's power of patronage so successfully that for the remaining seven years of the reign, he and his Norfolk neighbour and brother-in-law, Charles Viscount Townshend, virtually freed the king from all serious parliamentary opposition and enabled the country to grow rich without either internal or external strife.

GEORGE II

1727—1760

When George I died at sixty-four of a stroke during a visit to his beloved Hanover, it looked like the end of Walpole's monopoly of the royal ear. But the latter possessed a firm ally in the queen, Caroline of Anspach, by whom – for all his Teutonic obstinacy, pugnacity and meticulous attention to business and gallantry – the new King was ruled. So long as she lived the Prime Minister was secure in his exercise of the Crown's immense, though since 1688 limited, power. It rested on Parliament's readiness to grant the court and Government supply, to which Walpole provided the corollary by using the Crown's power of patronage to bribe a majority in the two Houses into acquiescence.

For the first twelve years of the reign, therefore, Walpole not only remained in power, but, in pursuit of his belief in public economy and distrust of foreign adventures, kept Britain at peace. But after the queen's death in 1737, parliamentary opposition to the Prime Minister built up round the rival royal establishment of the heir apparent at Leicester House, and, after the latter's death, of the Princess of Wales. Though the real aim of the intriguing Opposition magnates was to obtain office, their declared object was the abandonment of Walpole's cautious policy of avoiding war while retaining the king's favour by protecting his patrimony of Hanover with mercenaries hired by the British taxpayer. Instead they advocated a 'blue water' strategy of naval strength and oceanic commercial expansion at the expense of Spanish monopolists in South America and French trading and colonial settlements in Canada, India, West Africa and the West Indies. This was immensely popular with the City merchants, the middle class in the country and the London mob. But it would have made little impact on the built-in establishment of the Court and ministerial party in Parliament had it not been for the fiery genius of a great orator, William Pitt, member for the rotten borough of Old Sarum, who profoundly believed in it.

It was in Pitt's rise to power, against the bitter opposition of the Crown and political magnates, which made George II's reign one of the most exciting in British history. During the seventeen-forties, despite a victory won by George II in person at Dettingen, the French, with their superiority in population and internal resources, defeated the English and their allies at Fontenoy, overran Flanders, threatened England with invasion, financed a Jacobite rebellion in Scotland, captured the East India Company's trading station of Madras, and all but cut the British colonists in North America off from the continental interior. But in the last three years of the reign, thanks to Pitt, whom the old king had at last reluctantly admitted to power, a further war with France, which began in utter disaster, was transformed into a succession of unbelievable triumphs. It was won by Pitt's strategy of closely blockading the French naval ports while sending amphibious expeditions to attack the enemy's colonial settlements in every part of the world under young leaders chosen by him for qualities of daring and genius equal to his own. In 1757 a thirty-one-year-old former East India Company clerk, Robert Clive, with 900 British troops and 2000 native levies, routed an Indian army of 60,000 at Plassey, winning control of the three richest provinces of India. Two years later, another young general of Pitt's choosing, James Wolfe, stormed the Heights of Abraham to capture Quebec and posthumously assure the conquest of Canada. In that *annus mirabilis*, 1759, and the preceding and following years, Louisburg, Fort Duquesne, Goree, Senegal, Guadaloupe, Dominica, Montreal and Belle Isle all fell to British arms, while Hawke shattered a French fleet in Quiberon Bay, and six British infantry regiments covered themselves with glory at Minden. The entire nation responded to Pitt's inspired leadership. When in 1760 the old king died, his grandson, George III, echoing the country's new mood, began his reign by saying that he 'gloried in the name of Briton'.

GEORGE III

1760—1820

When, at twenty-two, George III succeeded his grandfather, he was immature, diffident and acutely conscious of his responsibilities and his inadequacy to bear them. Through bad luck, and partly through his deficiencies, this upright, emotional, conscientious, but pig-headed, prince became very unpopular. At the start of his reign he and his Minister, Lord Bute, alienated the commercial classes and the London mob by making a Peace which restored to France some of Pitt's conquests. Later he became involved in an unwise and humiliating prosecution of John Wilkes for libel which elevated that witty, but disreputable, adventurer into a popular champion of 'Liberty' against a royal tyrant suspected of seeking to restore Stuart despotism.

The climax of the king's unpopularity came when, in pursuit of a generally approved attempt to tax the American Colonies, he and his Minister, Lord North, so mismanaged matters that, not only did their stubborn legalism estrange the colonists beyond all hope of accommodation, but it brought about an armed intervention against Britain by all the maritime Powers of Europe. After a series of military disasters which all but ruined the country, the Navy just weathered the storm, and so, surprisingly, did the king, who at one moment was on the point of abdication. After being forced to accept a Ministry which stood for everything he detested, he was able, with considerable courage and political adroitness, to turn the tables on it, by using the odium it incurred over Fox's East India Bill to replace it by a minority Government under the twenty-four-year-old younger son and namesake of William Pitt, Earl of Chatham – until a General Election endorsed his choice.

Within five years of the loss of the American Colonies, the revival of prosperity under the brilliant young Minister whom he had so boldly placed in office brought about a national reaction in the king's favour. When in the autumn of 1788 the anxiety caused him by the extravagance and misconduct of his eldest son brought on an attack of insanity to an overstrained and never strong mind, sympathy for him became general. His convalescent pilgrimage to Weymouth after his recovery was a triumphal progress through flower-strewn villages and cheering crowds; at Lyndhurst, Fanny Burney recalled, the entire village accompanied the royal evening walk, repeatedly singing the National Anthem. 'The greatest conqueror' she wrote, 'could never pass through his dominions with fuller acclamations of joy from his devoted subjects than George III experienced, simply from having won their love by the even tenor of an unspotted life'. A faithful husband and devoted father – and, in his feckless eldest son, an injured one – the king had at last won the hearts of his people, not because he was their sovereign but because, being so, he was what they wanted him to be.

So it came about that during the long Revolutionary and Napoleonic Wars - which beginning in 1793, lasted, with two brief breaks, until the battle of Waterloo in 1815 - George III, for all his earlier unpopularity, proved a symbol of national unity and patriotism. His devotion to duty, the integrity of his life and his natural friendliness and good humour had turned him into an institution. In his familiar Windsor uniform – broad-skirted blue frock-coat with its scarlet collar and cuffs – and round hat, 'Old Nobbs' or 'Farmer George', as he was affectionately called, looked what he was, an English country gentleman. And when in 1811 – six years after Nelson's culminating victory of Trafalgar, which gave his country command of the world's seas for a century – his natural volubility degenerated into permanent and incurable insanity, it seemed to his people, not only a personal, but a national tragedy.

GEORGE IV

1820—1830

When in 1811, at the age of seventy-three, George III relapsed into final insanity, everyone expected that, on assuming the Regency, the Prince of Wales would dismiss his father's Tory Ministers and put his lifelong Whig friends in power. But the Whigs were a peace Party opposed to the war against Napoleon, then at long last entering its final phase, and were very unpopular. To their unspeakable fury, 'Prinny', as they called him, retained the Tories in office. By doing so he helped to ensure the continuance of Wellington's victories and postponed for a generation the Whig reform of a dangerously antiquated constitution.

Thirty years earlier, the Prince Regent, as he now became, had been the idol of society with, as Byron put it, 'fascination in his very bow', and the grace

'of being without alloy of fop or beau
A finished gentleman from top to toe'.

But age and self-indulgence had transformed him; his affability had grown vinous, and though he could still, on occasion, show an affecting affability and courtesy, he was Prince Charming no longer. He possessed an immense Hanoverian zest for life, could be, at times, a flamboyant, impulsive, overgrown baby, halloing over the supper-table, sobbing because his newest inamorata was cruel, or presiding over his private band, beating time on his thighs and accompanying himself at the top of his voice. But the gusto was degenerating into an irritable itch to domineer, and the surges of exuberant energy were succeeded by long periods of torpor, bile and self-pity. A younger generation, which had never known Prince Florizel, took a dark view of this epicurean veteran. To the young writers of the middle class who were to have the ear of the future, he seemed not merely the grotesque, flouncing, spoilt playboy whom his contemporaries remembered as a fairy-court prince, but as something far more sinister. To them he was Swellfoot the Tyrant who had betrayed the nascent cause of reform. The Radical poet, Leigh Hunt, described him in his weekly, *The Examiner*, as 'a libertine over head and ears in debt and disgrace, the companion of gamblers and demireps, who had just closed half a century without one single claim on the gratitude of his country'.

When George succeeded to the throne on the old mad king's death in 1820, he was trying, to the intense embarrassment of his Ministers, to divorce his wife – or, rather, one of his wives, for he had earlier morganatically married Mrs Fitzherbert. The queen's conduct had been as deplorable as his, but the scenes at her trial for adultery when, supported by an enthusiastic mob, she daily drove to the House of Lords, and her subsequent attempts to attend the Coronation, provided the scandal of the century and, but for her timely death, might have brought down the monarchy.

Yet this king, who proved such a national liability, had finer artistic taste than any English sovereign except, possibly, Richard II and Charles I. He knew more about architecture, painting, books and music than any prince in Europe, and left behind him, besides the furniture of his fantastic palaces, two of the world's finest examples of town planning – Regent's Street and Park, and Regency Brighton. They were his legacy to his country, yet few of his contemporaries appreciated them. They were far more interested in the Industrial Revolution, which, in his lifetime, had been changing the physical face of Britain and enhancing the wealth and livelihood of her people. It was during his reign that there occurred the first scene of a still greater social transformation – the opening in 1825 of the Stockton–Darlington Railway, which, with Stephenson's famous 'Rocket' of 1829, heralded the coming of the Railway Age.

WILLIAM IV

1830—1837

For ten years the throne had been occupied by a gross, spoilt, self-indulgent roué who, in order to avoid the gaze of his disapproving subjects, spent the end of his reign in almost complete seclusion in a luxurious cottage in Windsor Forest, where he divided his time between lying in bed, playing whist with his mistress, fishing in Virginia Water, designing new uniforms for the Army, and making things as difficult as he could for his Ministers. His final contribution to politics was to delay as long as possible – on allegedly conscientious grounds – his assent to an Act of Catholic Emancipation which the Government considered essential for the peace of a dangerously disturbed Ireland, and which his father, out of deference to his Coronation Oath, had refused the younger Pitt a quarter of a century earlier.

George IV was succeeded by his sailor brother, William IV – formerly Duke of Clarence – whose chief claims to distinction were to have served in early life with Nelson, to have mildly Whig sympathies, and to have enjoyed for many years the domestic companionship of the famous actress, Mrs Jordan, by whom – before he dismissed her in the vain hope of producing legitimate progeny – he had a large illegitimate brood. He was, in the words of Lytton Strachey, 'a bursting, bubbling old gentleman, with quarter-deck gestures, round rolling eyes and a head like a pineapple,' who achieved a brief, precarious popularity through his bluff habit of spontaneous speech with everyone – often of the most embarrassingly indiscreet kind – and by his Ministers's feat, commemorated in the pot-house ballad, of having 'bated the tax upon beer'.

He needed all the popularity he could get, for the long-delayed storm, which had been threatening an unreformed Britain, broke at the outset of his reign. It saw the fall from office of the Tories who, with one brief interval, had governed Britain for nearly forty years, and the destruction, on a wave of agitation and rioting, of the old parliamentary constitution of oligarchic power and privilege, rotten boroughs and balanced powers which had provided the country's rulers since the Revolution of 1688. By the Reform Bill, which the Whigs, with the King's help, passed in 1832, and the Municipal Reform Bill of 1834, ultimate political power, though for the present mainly under aristocratic leadership, was transferred to the fast-rising middle classes of the capital and the industrial North and Midlands, with their Utilitarian belief in laissez-faire, the career open to the talents, and freedom of trade.

The House of Windsor

VICTORIA

1837—1901

In the hungry and divisive years after Waterloo, when an aged, crazed, blind king wandered, with long, unkempt white beard, through the deserted rooms of Windsor Castle, one of his disreputable and heirless sons discarded a long-loved mistress and, in order to get Parliament to pay his debts, married a German princess. In 1819, shortly before his own death, there was born to the Duke of Kent a daughter, christened Victoria, who, during the brief reigns of her two unprepossessing uncles, grew up – in the rural seclusion of Kensington Palace under the tutelage of her widowed mother – the one hope on which the continuance of the Hanoverian dynasty and the English Crown seemed to depend. For at that time most progressive and liberal-minded men believed that hereditary monarchy was an irrational and obstructive anachronism and that, following the example of the United States, Britain would soon be a republic.

The young princess who at the age of eighteen ascended the throne was to prove them wrong. On the day on which, arrayed in her nightgown, she learnt at 6 a.m. from the kneeling Archbishop of Canterbury and Lord Chamberlain that she was Queen, she wrote in her diary:

> Since it had pleased Providence to place me in this station I shall do my utmost to fulfil my duties towards my country. I am very young and perhaps in many, though not in all things, inexperienced, but I am sure that very few have more real good-will and more real desire to do what is fit and right than I have.

For this youthful inheritor of an imperilled monarchical tradition, though no genius, was a woman of conscience and character. 'I will be good', she is reported to have said when first told of her future destiny.

Her sixty-four years' reign saw immense social and political changes. At its start the population of the British Isles was about 25 millions, at its end more than 41 millions, and this despite the

Irish Famine of 1846 and the mass emigration which halved the population of Ireland. The transformation of national wealth and habit was even greater; before the Queen died the British had become a predominantly urban and industrial people, dependent on ocean imports and manufactured exports, and no longer on their own fields.

Yet through all the immense changes of Victoria's reign, the national standards of honour, behaviour and self-help remained a constant factor, transcending differences of class, wealth, creed and politics. They animated the cloth-capped Socialist and Trade Union agitator of the later years of the reign as much as the top-hatted Utilitarians of its earlier years. They were largely set by a Court whose royal mistress represented her subjects' moral convictions and aspirations. The great Victorians – in statesmanship, science, industry, literature, philanthropy, exploration and war – were as appropriately linked with the name of their Sovereign as the great Elizabethans had been with theirs.

So, in a sense, were the peoples of the vast multi-racial empire over which Victoria presided as Queen Empress, covering by the end of her reign nearly a quarter of the habitable globe and of its inhabitants. At her Diamond Jubilee in 1897 a vast military thanksgiving parade was held in London, with proud contingents drawn from every continent in the world. At the centre of that glittering procession, driving through dense, cheering crowds in an open carriage to St Paul's, was the little old lady in black in whose name all this pageantry was enacted. 'From my heart', ran her message at the day's end, 'I thank my beloved people. May God bless them!'

EDWARD VII

1901—1910

The long-deferred nine years' reign of Edward VII was an anti-climax to Victorian rectitude and earnestness, but it was, at least for the prosperous – and it was an age of prosperity – a very jolly, luxurious and carefree one while it lasted. The monarch, hirsute, convival and a little guttural, was immensely popular with his subjects. Though war clouds were gathering abroad – where the King's nephew, Kaiser William, by his neurotic indiscretions and sword-wavings, was keeping Europe in a series of recurrent crises – and a strongly radical Liberal Government took over power in 1905, the spirit of the reign was best epitomized by the Ritz Hotel, the Daimler car, and the song which proclaimed,

> There ain't going to be no war,
> Not with a king like good King Teddy,
> 'E don't like that sort of thing.

This genial sovereign, who succeeded in his sixty-second year, had suffered from an over-disciplined youth owing to the excessive thoroughness with which his high-minded Teutonic father, Prince Albert, supervised his education, and the moral puritanical strait-jacket in which both his parents had kept him lest he should take after his rakish great-uncles. The result was that, as soon as he could escape the parental leading-strings, he had proceeded to have as good a time as he was able. This made him, with his beautiful Danish wife, Princess Alexandra, the leader of fashionable society, but caused his mother, who strongly disapproved of his goings-on, to deny him any share in the exercise of her constitutional functions.

None the less, when his time at last came, Edward, who had great shrewdness, humanity and understanding of his fellow men, justified, and more than justified, his brief tenure of the throne. For it was his bonhomie and good humour, his refusal to be petty and take offence at insults, and above all, his undisguised love of France, which captured the hearts of Parisians and the French people. His service to the cause of Anglo-French understanding was that he changed the popular – or, rather, until that time, unpopular – image of England in France and presented it, not as a starched and designing hypocrisy, but as something warm-hearted, enjoying and appreciative. As he said at a banquet at the Elysée palace, his great desire was that the two nations might march together in the path of civilization and peace. His reward was the Entente Cordiale, which he did so much to bring about and which, after his death, helped to save the liberties of Europe from an otherwise irresistible German militarism.

GEORGE V

1910—1936

George V, like his great-great-grandfather, George III, was essentially a good man, with a deep sense of the responsibilities of a constitutional monarch. Unlike George III he was not handicapped by the neurotic fears which put such a tragic strain on that monarch. He owed much to the happy, loving home life which his wise father, mindful of his own over-disciplined upbringing, and his mother, Queen Alexandra, gave him, and to his early training as a sailor, begun at the age of twelve. In the old *Britannia* and in a voyage round the world in the frigate *Bacchante*, he received neighbour's fare, sharing the hard life of the sea under sail. Before he was seventeen he had learnt what it was to be cold and hungry, to climb the rigging, to face mountainous seas, to obey as well as to give orders.

Having, as a younger son, no thought of the throne, he made the Navy his profession, serving in turn as midshipman, lieutenant, commander and acting-captain until his twenty-seventh year, when the death of his elder brother placed him in direct succession to the Crown. Later, as Duke of York and Prince of Wales, he fulfilled the public duties which fall to the lot of a royal prince, visiting Australia, New Zealand, South Africa, Canada, India and Burma and acquiring a deep feeling for the vast, world-wide empire which had been growing up almost unrealized by people at home. In all this he was assisted by his wife and cousin, Mary of Teck, one of the most remarkable women of her age, with a deep understanding of her country's history and heritage.

It was no easy charge which King George assumed in 1910, after the brief hedonistic reign of Edward VII. Lords and Commons were on the verge of battle, with the Government appealing to the nation for powers to change the constitution and invoking the royal prerogative to enable it to do so. Labour unrest seemed darkening into what well might end in revolution, the Protestant Irish of Ulster were threatening civil war rather than accept Catholic majority rule, and a half-crazed German war-lord, backed by the world's greatest army, was posturing perilously on the brink of Armageddon. All the while the shipyards of Germany and Britain resounded with hammering, as dreadnought after dreadnought rose in the stocks against the global struggle to come.

For four years of warfare, while the British people created behind their traditional shield of sea-power a volunteer army which, at the cost of a million lives, ultimately broke the German will for conquest, King George symbolized, by his character and selfless performance of duty, the nation's sacrifice and resolve. And when, in war's aftermath, chaos followed abroad, and at home old standards ceased to be honoured, the straightforward consistency, dignity and flawless conduct of the king and queen proved an oasis of example for reviving sanity and decency. More perhaps than by any other influence, the change of opinion during the last decade of the reign was brought about by the personal example of the Throne. Quietly and unobtrusively its occupants made ordinary men and women feel that the Crown was being worn for their service. They brought the throne into the street and made contact between its gilded majesty and the drab dwellings of workaday Britain. Through the restless years of social division before and after the First World War, ran an unobtrusive but persistent undertone of royal endeavour. It was directed not towards power or political influence but towards a greater understanding of the needs of an industrial people over whom the royal couple, for all the limitations of constitutional monarchy, were called upon to preside. For King George's subjects, and particularly the humbler ones, were learning to realize that they had a big asset in their king. He might not be a showy man, but he was a good and honest one. He came among them – a plain Englishman with a conscience and heart who, like them, had learnt a working craft when he was young and never to let the sun go down on a task which the day should have seen fulfilled.

EDWARD VIII

1936

Edward VIII's reign was the shortest in English history, excepting those of Harold and Edward V. It was a dynastic tragedy which somehow, through the curious British capacity for getting the best of both worlds, ended in something rather less than a tragedy for its two chief participants, the King and the British people. For the former gained the lifelong partnership he needed, and the latter retained their hereditary monarchy.

The Prince of Wales, as he became in 1910 on his sixteenth birthday, was the victim, in a near-revolutionary age, of a generation gap. His father, whose unshakable constancy in war and peace remained a sheet-anchor to his country, was firmly rooted in the conventional beliefs and behaviour of the pre-1914 world. The prince was not, for he belonged to a generation whose members found themselves between 1914 and 1918 submerged in warfare of unimaginable – to those who never experienced it – horror and suffering. Forbidden for dynastic reasons to join his regiment in the front line, in which he would probably have been killed, he served throughout those four apocalyptic years with the armies in France, trying on every possible occasion, and as constantly being prevented, to join his comrades and contemporaries in their long heroic martyrdom.

It was with this war generation that the prince identified himself and was identified. When the long nightmare ended those of its survivors in a position to do so not unnaturally sought such pleasure as they could find, sometimes in ways which outraged the conventions and moral attitudes of their elders who had not undergone their shattering experience. Nowhere was that generation gap of incomprehension wider than between the wearer of the Crown and the Heir Apparent. That the latter should settle down and marry a suitable princess as his forerunners had done seemed to King George an inescapable obligation of his position, while to his son it was anathema, believing as he did, like all his generation, that a man should be free to follow the dictates of his heart. It was to a married American lady, with a divorced husband living, that these ultimately led him.

When King George died in January 1936 his successor was faced with a terrible dilemma. As king he was Head of the Church of England by whose rites he would have to be crowned and one of whose tenets was the indissolubility of Christian marriage. Yet he knew that the loneliness and solitude of his position would be unbearable without the support and consolation of the one woman he loved and whom, when she had divorced her second husband, he was determined to marry. It was Edward's virtue – as it was of the Prime Minister, Stanley Baldwin, who acted as the honest broker between him and the nation – that he saw clearly that the chivalrous course he had chosen was bound to divide instead of uniting, as the Crown was meant to, the country and Commonwealth. The only solution by which he could safeguard the national inheritance of hereditary monarchy was to abdicate and let his brother, with his happy marriage and family, take his place.

So it came about, at a time when great tempests were blowing up from a dark international horizon, that the young king who, as Heir Apparent, had done great public service and made himself loved throughout the Commonwealth, voluntarily vacated his throne before he could be crowned. With a touching simplicity he made his renunciation; nor did anything in his brilliant, generous, but erratic, career become him like the leaving of it.

GEORGE VI

1936—1952

George VI perfectly symbolized the endurance and courage of a sadly buffeted British generation. When he was eighteen and the First World War broke out, he went to sea, serving at Jutland, the most important naval engagement since Trafalgar. Later he became one of the first officers of the new Fighting Service to which the 1914-18 War gave birth, the Royal Air Force.

In 1936, after serving his country with unassuming conscientiousness as Duke of York, he was unexpectedly called to the throne. Utterly distasteful as it was to him to take a beloved brother's place, he showed complete abnegation of self, sacrificing, with a dignity which concealed all show of self-sacrifice, his personal wishes, and shouldering, despite a painful handicap of speech, the interminable burdens and tasks of kingship. Two years after he was crowned the storm of war again broke over Europe. By 1940 the British people stood alone facing the greatest menace of their history. Instinctively, they looked to the Throne. They were not disappointed. The king, with his devoted consort and their children, remained, resolute and imperturbable, at the post of danger and duty. All Britons knew that under no conceivable circumstances would their Sovereign – the symbol of their courage and unity – falter or parley with the foe. Like his Minister, Winston Churchill, he embodied and stood for all the ancient, enduring virtues of his country. By his steadiness he helped to give the British people that unshakeable confidence which astonished and ultimately restored a breaking world. As the Stukas dived on his Palace, the clerks and typists making their comfortless way to their daily tasks amid scenes of desolation and destruction, and the working folk who stood, bloody but unbowed, among the ruins of their homes and household goods, instinctively stiffened with pride. The King of England was on the throne of his fathers; like the great Elizabeth, he would not be by violence constrained.

Four years later, in June 1944, King George watched the sailing of the great British-American armada which was to liberate western Europe. It was the epitome of his reign. This quiet, kindly, courageous man and the people he and his queen so worthily represented had withstood the worst that Fate could bring against them, and, enduring all things in the confidence of the righteousness of their cause, had prepared for four years for this day, leaving no stone unturned that could assure success. They who, through their good nature and trust in the intentions of others, had been so weak, had made themselves strong, not because they admired or sought strength for its own sake, but because they had found that there was no other way by which they could defend and preserve their ideals.

In 1945, on VE Day and on VJ Day, the triumph of those ideals over both the Nazis and Japanese was consummated. On each of these occasions the people turned to the Throne, surrounding the Palace to acclaim their king and queen. Many of the high, and perhaps foolish, hopes of that time of liberation and victory were falsified by later events. But though wickedness – tyranny, greed, intolerance and bad faith – as in other generations, survived the defeat of the wicked, the king's life, in peace as in war, continued to remind his subjects of the ideals for which they had fought and suffered. In his keeping, as in his father's, the Crown stood for the virtues which from age to age restrain the forces of evil – truth, gentleness, loving kindness, courage in affliction, strength in adversity, tenderness to the weak, constancy to pledged word and duty. Destined like his generation to inherit an iron age, King George passed through the fire unscathed and, in the crowded, terrible years of his short but momentous reign, never uttered a word or performed an act which was not worthy of the traditions of his country's ancient and Christian Throne.

ELIZABETH II

1952—

When Elizabeth succeeded her father at the age of twenty-five, the British Commonwealth, of which she was titular head, covered a quarter of the earth's habitable surface, while its population exceeded a quarter of the human race. The two Rhodesias, Malta, Malaya, Singapore, Jamaica and the British West Indian Islands, Kenya, Nigeria, Uganda, Tanganyika, the Sudan, Nyasaland, Zanzibar, the Gold Coast, and Somaliland were still British Colonies or Protectorates. Today, a process begun in the reign of the queen's father has been virtually completed, and nearly all Britain's former dominions and dependencies have been granted full independence and national sovereignty, together with generous financial and other aid. No comparable act of liberation by the rulers of a great Empire is known to history. In place of the former British Empire there is now a multi-racial Commonwealth of independent Sovereign States, in which Britain is, at best, only *primus inter pares*.

Yet despite contraction abroad and inflation and over-population at home, and a growing concentration of power in the hands of giant Government Departments, financial Corporations and Trade Unions at the expense of personal liberty and independence, Queen Elizabeth's subjects in the first two decades of her reign contrived to endow the world with some of its most remarkable inventions – the jump-jet, the hovercraft, carbon-fibre, float-glass, the saving drugs Cephalorspin and Celbenin, and the fuel-cell which made the American moon-flights possible. And notwithstanding a vast influx of new subjects from lands without Britain's long democratic tradition and experience, and a steady increase in crimes of violence and road accidents, in no major country in the world is life for the majority safer, freer or more kindly.

Yet if there has been some public disillusion during the reign with Britain's political and administrative institutions and rulers, there has been little or none with the Crown. And for this, in a jealously egalitarian age, the credit belongs to the wearer of the

Crown and the devotion and efficiency with which, in the face of unceasing publicity, the Queen and Royal Family have carried out their duties. One reason why British constitutional monarchy has worked so well in the fast-changing third quarter of the twentieth century has been the queen's clear grasp of its place and purpose in the modern State and the absolute self-dedication she has shown in filling it. Superbly fitted by upbringing, training, character and self-discipline for her exacting and unique task, not the least of her services to the country has been the way in which she and the Duke of Edinburgh have brought up their children to follow in her footsteps.

The legal and spiritual association of men of different creeds, races, callings and classes in a nation, though often taken for granted, is a more wonderful miracle of human effort and ingenuity than the greatest achievement of science. For it enables millions who have never set eyes on one another to act together in peace and mutual trust. In Britain it is the monarchy, though long divested of political responsibility, which reminds men that the political and economic differences which divide them are less real than the ties of history and common service which unite them.

The Queen does not only symbolize, and help to promote, the unity of her people. She serves to remind them of their ideals. She represents in her person and family life, and in her dedication to her public duties, the abiding virtues of hearth, home and service on the foundations of which society rests. She brings, in Burke's phrase, 'the dispositions that are lovely in private life into the service and conduct of the commonwealth'. In that transfigured moment during her coronation – witnessed not only by the vast congregation in the Abbey but, through the miracle of television, by millions of her subjects throughout the world – she was bidden in God's name to 'do justice, stop the growth of iniquity, protect the Holy Church of God, help and defend widows and orphans, restore the things that are gone to decay, maintain the things that are restored, punish and reform what is amiss and confirm what is in good order'. By the example set from the throne, by the sincerity of her self-dedication to her unique and lonely task of serving her subjects all the days of her life, the Queen is the guarantee under God that those who direct the destinies of the nation will endeavour in her name to do those things.

LANCASTER

HENRY IV = Mary de Bohun
1399 -1413

Owen Tudor = Catherine of France = HENRY V
1413 -1422

HENRY VI
1422 -1461

Edmund Tudor

TUDOR

HEN
1485

James IV of Scotland = Margaret Tudor

Kathe

James V of Scotland = Marie de Guise

Mary Queen of Scots = Henry Lord Darnley

JAMES I = Anne of Denmark
1603 -1625

CHARLES I = Henrietta Maria
1625 -1649

Interregn

CHARLES II
1660 -1685

JAMES II = Anne Hyde
1685 -1688

Mary = William of Oran

MARY II = WILLIAM III
1689 -1694   1689 -1702

ANNE
1702 -1714

HANOVER

GEORGE IV
1820 -1830

W

G

EDWARD VIII
1936